SCIENCE-FICTION
MOVIES

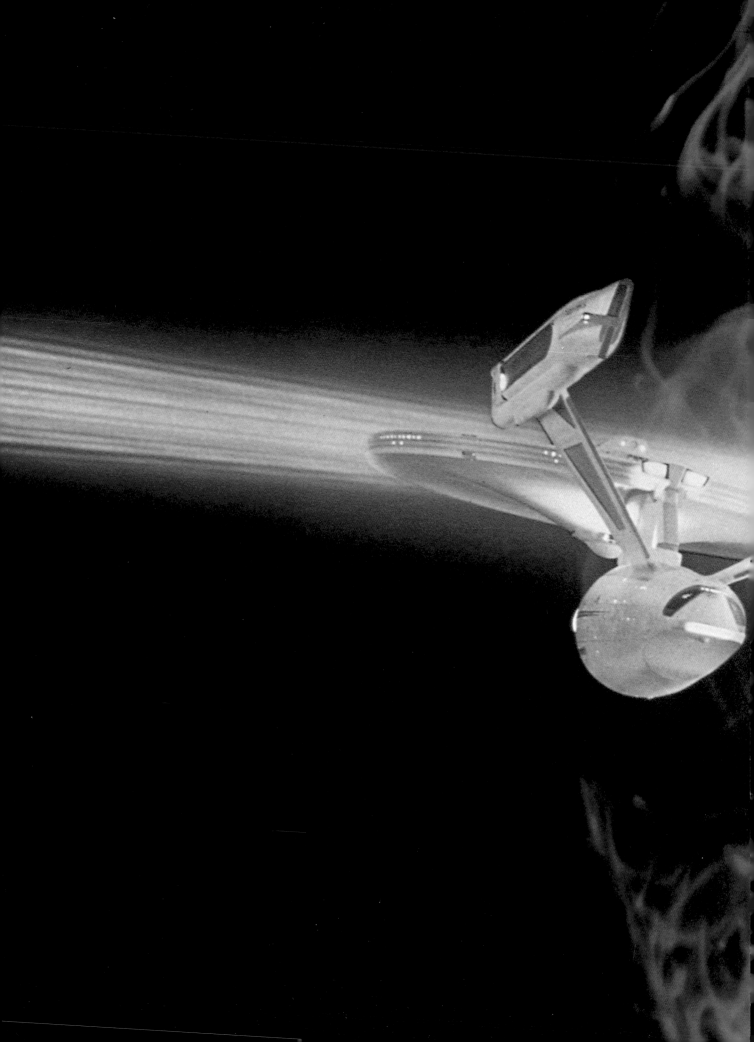

SCIENCE-FICTION
MOVIES

ILLUSTRATED REVIEWS OF THE CLASSIC FILMS

HAMLYN

Half-title page: *Herbert Berghof, Peter Graves and Andrea King study a star chart in* **Red Planet Mars.**

Title pages: *The Starship Enterprise and its crew make another journey in* **Star Trek V The Final Frontier**

ACKNOWLEDGMENTS
Editor: Julian Brown
Design Editor: Leigh Jones
Designer: Tony Truscott
Jacket designer: Ashley Western
Production Controller: Nick Thompson
Picture researcher: Jenny Faithfull

Photographic acknowledgments
Ronald Grant Archive 10-11, 17 top, 18, 19, 21, 23, 24, 27, 30, 32-33, 32 bottom, 36, 38, 39 top, 39 bottom, 40, 41, 43, 45, 50-51, 54, 55, 57 top, 61, 62, 64, 66-67, 71, 74, 75, 76, 88, 93, 95, 101, 102, 110, 111, 112, 115, 120, 121, 122, 123, 124-125; Kobal Collection 1, 4-5, 6, 8, 9, 12, 14-15, 17 bottom, 22, 25, 28, 42, 46, 48, 52, 57 bottom, 59, 65, 77 bottom, 78, 79, 80, 81, 82, 84, 86, 87, 90-91, 92, 94 top, 94 bottom, 96, 97, 98, 99, 104-105, 108, 109, 113 left, 113 right, 114, 116 bottom, 127, 128; Octopus Publishing Group Ltd 16, 26, 58, 68, 72-73, 77 top, 83, 103, 107, 116 top, 118-119.

Published in 1992
by The Hamlyn Publishing Group Limited
part of Reed International Books
Michelin House, 81 Fulham Road, London SW3 6RB

Copyright © 1992 Variety Inc.

ISBN 0 600 57488 1

A catalogue record for this book is available from the British Library

Produced by Mandarin Offset
Printed in China.

GLOSSARY

The following is a guide to 80 years of *Variety* 'slanguage' as occurs in the reviews selected; it is not exhaustive and is intended especially for non-American and more general readers.

Variety's snazzy coinages are a goulash of publishing and showbiz/movie jargon, foreign words, Yiddish, street slang, contractions and acronyms that since the mid-1930s have since acquired a reputation and life of their own.

Many of the words have long vanished from use in the paper (along with the slang that inspired them); new ones are still being invented by writers. The only rule is that they sound 'right' and carry on the tradition of sharp, tabloid, flavourful prose.

As a further aid for general readers we have also included some words that are simple movie jargon or archaic slang rather than pure *Variety* language.

a.k.	ass-kisser	helm(er)	direct(or)	org	organization	stepping	dancing
a.k.a.	also known as	histrionics	performance(s)	ozoner	drive-in theatre	stew	drinking bout
ankle	alcoholic	histrionically	performance-wise	p.a.	press agent	sudser	soap opera
anent	regarding	hoke	hokum	pactee	contract player	super	super-production
avoirdupois	weight	hoke up	over-act	Par	Paramount	switcheroo	(plot) twist
b.b.	big business	hoofology	dancing	pen	penitentiary;	tab	tabloid
beer stube	bar	hotcha	excellent		prison	tapster	tap-dancer
belter	boxer	hoyden(ish)	tomboy(ish)	Pennsy	Pennsylvania	ten-twent-thirt/10-20-30	
burley	burlesque, music	ink	sign	photog	photographer		amateurish (acting)
	hall	i.r.	inquiring or inves	pic	picture; movie	terp(ing)	danc(ing)
bow	debut; praise		tigative reporter	plat	platinum blonde	terpsichore	dancing
b.r.	bankroll; sum of	jitterbug	(1940s) jazz	p.m.	professional	thesp(ing)	actor, act(ing)
	money		dance(r); nervous		model	thespically	performance-wise
cannon	gun		person	p.o.v.	point of view	thespics	acting
carny	carnival	kayo	knockout	p.r.	public relations	tint(ed)	colour(ed)
Chi	Chicago	legit(imate)	theatrical, theatre,	prexy	(company) presi-	tintuner	showbiz musical
chili	Mexican		stage		dent	topkick	boss
chirp(er)	sing(er)	legiter	stage play	profesh	profession	topper	boss
chopsocky	martial arts (film)	legituner	stage musical	programmer	B-movie fodder	topline(r)	star
chore	job; routine	lense(r)	photograph(er)	pug	boxer	trick work	special effects
	assignment	limn	portray	quondam	one time	trouping	acting
chump	crazy (in love)	lingo	dialogue	ridic	ridiculous	tube	TV
cleff(er)	compose(r)	longhair	intellectual; high	rod-man	gunman	20th	20th Century-Fox
click	hit; success		brow	RR	railroad; railway	U	Universal
coin	money; finance	lower case	minor (quality)	s.a.	sex appeal	unreel	play
contempo	contemporary	manse	mansion	sauce	alcohol	unspool	play
d.a.	district attorney	meg(aphoner)	direct(or)	schtick	comic routine(s)	upper case	major (quality)
dick	detective	megger	director	scripter	scriptwriter	vaude	vaudeville
doughboy	infantry soldier	meller	melodrama(tic)	sec	secretary	vet	veteran
dualer	double-billed	milquetoast	meek man	sheet	screen; news-	vignetting	describing
	feature film	nabes	suburbs		paper	vis-a-vis	(romantic/sexual/
femme	female; woman	negative cost	production cost	shutterbug	photographer		billing) partner
flap	flapper	nitery	nightclub	slugfest	fight	warbling	singing
flivver	car	oater	Western	smokeater	fireman	WB	Warner Bros.
gat	gun	ofay	white man	sock(eroo)	excellent; power-	w.k.	well-known
gob	sailor	oke	okay		ful	yahoo	redneck
Gotham	New York	one-shot	one-off	solon	lawmaker	yak	joke
gyp	swindler; cheat	o.o.	once-over	speak	speakeasy	yclept	played by
habiliments	clothing	opp	opposite	spec	spectacle	yock	joke

SCIENCE-FICTION MOVIES

CONTENTS

INTRODUCTION

Variety is the world's premier entertainment newspaper. Founded in 1905, its film reviews run from 1907 and cover virtually the entire history of 20th-century cinema, with the freshness both of reviews written at the time of release and of *Variety*'s incisive house style.

Comedy Movies is a collection of over 300 reviews of some of the most memorable comedy films of all time. Because of space, the selection has been limited to movies made in the English language. In editing the reviews down (often from many times their original length) much detail has unavoidably been lost. But we have tried to preserve the useful basics – a snappy intro, plot essentials, assessments of the main performances and technical merits, and any interesting background.

Reviewers' box-office predictions have been cut out, as well as plot revelations. Minor changes have been made so that the reviews 'read' from a modern viewpoint, and any now-meaningless contemporary references and prejudices (especially during the two world wars and the McCarthy period) have been toned down or deleted.

Any rewriting has been kept to the absolute minimum to preserve the flavour and opinions of the originals, although until the mid-1930s, when *Variety* reviews began to take on their current shape, editing has had to be considerably heavier.

American spellings and *Variety*'s 'language' have been retained (see Glossary); any annotations to the reviews have been put in square brackets. Although *Variety* recently began to include accents on foreign names, this book adheres to tradition by omitting them.

Assembling credits for each film has often involved extra research, and this in turn has been limited by the usual constraints of time and money. *Variety* only started regularly to publish cast lists and limited technical credits in the mid-1920s; fuller credits began from the late 1930s. Mistakes and misprints have been corrected where possible; real names put in square brackets after pseudonyms; and the latest version of people's names used throughout for consistency in the present format.

The following are the main criteria used:

★ **Film title** The original title in country of origin (or 'majority' country, in the case of co-productions). The form of the title is that used on the print itself, not that on secondary material like posters or press handouts. Subsidiary titles (a growing trend since the 1980s) are put on a separate line. Films are listed in strict A-Z order, letter by letter, ignoring all word-breaks and punctuation; those starting with numerals are positioned as if the figures were spelt out. All films included have received a theatrical showing at some time in their life.

★ **Year** The year of first public release in its country of origin (or, with co-productions, 'majority' country). Sneaks, out-of-town tryouts and festival screenings don't count; end-of-year Oscar-qualifying runs do. Establishing some films' opening dates is still problematical.

★ **Running time** The hardest nut to crack. Except when it's obvious the reviewer has been shown a rough-cut, *Variety*'s original running times are used. For silent films a very approximate conversion has been made, based on the number of reels or on information contained in the review. Films tend to get shorter over the years as they're trimmed, cut for TV and generally mangled; more recently there has been a trend towards issuing longer versions for TV or video. No running time should be taken as gospel.

★ **Colour** All films in colour, partly in colour, or tinted carry the symbol ◇. Some in the last two categories are now only shown in black-and-white but still carry the colour symbol as this denotes their original form,

★ **Silent** Where a film was made without sound it is indicated with the symbol ⊗.

★ **Video** A nightmare, Films which have been released on video (at one time or another) carry the following symbols: ⊗ = available in both the US and the UK; ⊗ = available in the US only; and ⊗ = available in the UK only. But given the differences from country to country, and the rapid pace of deletions, don't necessarily expect to find a copy in your local store. Catalogue numbers are of little practical use, so have not been included.

★ **Director** The film's officially credited director or co-directors. Some productions are in fact the work of several hands (especially during Hollywood's studio era); only well-known uncredited contributions are noted in square brackets. Second unit or dance-number directors are occasionally included if their contribution merits it.

★ **Country of origin** The second hardest nut. The rule here has been where the money actually came from, rather than where a film was shot, what passport the director had, or what language the cast spoke in. With co-productions, the first country listed is the 'majority' one (which decides its official title – see above). In the case of many British and American movies, especially since the 1950s, deciding whether some are UK/US, US/UK, or even UK or US is virtually impossible.

★ **Cast lists** For space reasons, these have been limited to a maximum of six, not necessarily in their original order of billing. Early appearances by later stars are often included for interest's sake, even though they may only be bit-parts. For consistency, actors who later changed names are listed by their latest moniker.

★ **Academy awards/nominations** The date is that of the Oscar award not of the ceremony (generally held the following spring).

Wanted murderer Bob Peck (on top of the aeroplane) is captured by Bill Paxton and taken down the Slipstream.

THE ABYSS

1989, 140 mins, ◇ Ⓥ *Dir* James Cameron   US

★ *Stars* Ed Harris, Mary Elizabeth Mastrantonio, Michael Biehn, Leo Burmester, Todd Graff, Kimberley Scott

A first-rate underwater suspenser with an otherworldly twist, *The Abyss* suffers from a payoff unworthy of its buildup. Same sensibilities that enable writer-director James Cameron to deliver riveting, supercharged action segments get soggy when the 'aliens' turn out to be friendly.

Action is launched when a navy nuclear sub suffers a mysterious power failure and crashes into a rock wall. Bud Brigman (Ed Harris) and his gamy crew of undersea oil-rig workers are hired to dive for survivors.

At the last minute Brigman's flinty estranged wife, Lindsey (Mary Elizabeth Mastrantonio), who designed their submersible oil rig, insists on coming aboard to lend an un-invited hand.

Crew finds nothing but a lot of corpses floating eerily in the water-filled sub, but meanwhile, Lindsey has a close encounter with a kind of swift-moving neon-lit jellyfish she's convinced is a friendly alien. When turbulence from a hurricane rocking the surface cuts off the crew's ties to their command ship, their underwater stay is perilously extended.

The Abyss has plenty of elements in its favor, not least the performances by Harris as the compassionate crewleader and Mastrantonio as his steel-willed counterpart. Not even the $50 million-plus pic's elaborate technical achievements can overshadow these two..

THE ADVENTURES OF BARON MUNCHAUSEN

1989, 125 mins, ◇ Ⓥ *Dir* Terry Gilliam   UK, W. GERMANY

★ *Stars* John Neville, Eric Idle, Sarah Polley, Oliver Reed, Charles McKeown

A fitting final installment in Terry Gilliam's trilogy begun with *Time Bandits* and continued with *Brazil*, *The Adventures of Baron Munchausen* shares many of those films' strengths and weaknesses, but doesn't possess the visionary qualities of the latter.

*Submarine sci-fi: close encounters of an underwater kind when oil divers enter **The Abyss**.*

The film offers a continual feast for the eyes, and not enough for the funnybone or the heart. Set in Europe in the 18th century, tale begins with a city under intense siege by the Turks. An elderly gent who purports to be the Baron begins relating the true story of how he caused he war.

With this, Gilliam takes the viewer into the exquisite palace of the sultan, whose ferocity is aroused when he loses a bet to the visiting Baron (John Neville). With the help of his variously and superhumanly gifted gang of four, which consists of the fastest runner in the world, a dwarf who can exhale with hurricane force, an expert sharpshooter and an immeasurably strong black man, the Baron makes off with the sultan's entire treasure, but his city is left to suffer the consequences.

Promising to save the city from the renewed attack, the Baron escapes in a gigantic hot-air baloon fashioned out of ladies' underwear, and goes in search of his four comrades. This journey takes the unlikely pair to some unlikely places where they meet some unlikely people.

THE ADVENTURES OF BUCKAROO BANZAI, ACROSS THE 8TH DIMENSION

1984, 103 mins, ◇ Ⓥ *Dir* W.D. Richter   US

★ *Stars* Peter Weller, John Lithgow, Ellen Barkin, Jeff Goldblum, Christopher Lloyd, Rosalind Cash

The Adventures of Buckaroo Banzai plays more like an experimental film than a Hollywood production aimed at a mass audience. It violates every rule of storytelling and narrative structure in creating a world of its own.

First-time director W.D. Richter and writer Earl Mac Rauch have here created a comic book world chock full of references, images, pseudo scientific ideas and plain mumbo jumbo.

Buried within all this Banzai trivia is an indecipherable plot involving a modern band of Robin Hoods who go to battle with enemy aliens released accidentally from the eighth dimension as a result of Buckaroo's experiments with particle physics.

Buckaroo is a world-class neurosurgeon, physicist, race car driver and, with his band of merry pranksters, the Hong Kong Cavaliers, a rock 'n' roll star.

As the great one (Buckaroo), Peter Weller presents a moving target that is tough to hit. Also very funny is Jeff Goldblum, coming as if from another dimension as every mother's Jewish son. Ellen Barkin does a turn as Buckaroo's mysterious girlfriend and looks great but is another emotionless character.

ALIEN

1979, 124 mins, ◇ Ⓥ *Dir* Ridley Scott   US

★ *Stars* Tom Skerritt, Sigourney Weaver, Veronica Cartwright, Harry Dean Stanton, John Hurt, Ian Holm

Plainly put, *Alien* is an old-fashioned scary movie set in a highly realistic sci-fi future, made all the more believable by expert technical craftmanship.

Script has more loose ends than the Pittsburgh Steelers but that doesn't matter as director Ridley Scott, cameraman Derek Vanlint and composer Jerry Goldsmith propel the emotions relentlessly from one visual surprise – and horror – to the next.

The price paid for the excitement, and it's a small one,

Inter-dimensional hokum as roadster/rock star Buckaroo battles the aliens in **The Adventures of Buckaroo Banzai.**

is that there is very little involvement with the characters themselves.

Alien initially presents a mundane commercial space-craft with crew members like Yaphet Kotto bitching and moaning about wages and working conditions.

The tedium is shared by captain Tom Skerritt, his aide Sigourney Weaver and the rest of the crew, played by a generally good cast in cardboard roles.

Eventually, it is Weaver who gets the biggest chance and she carries it off well.

ALIENS

1986, 137 mins, ◇ ⓥ *Dir* James Cameron   US

★ *Stars* Sigourney Weaver, Carrie Henn, Michael Biehn, Lance Henricksen, Paul Reiser, Jenette Goldstein

Aliens proves a very worthy followup to Ridley Scott's 1979 sci-fi shocker, *Alien*. James Cameron's vault into the big time after scoring with the exploitation actioner *The Terminator* makes up for lack of surprise with sheer volume of thrills and chills – emphasis is decidedly on the plural aspect of the title.

Cameron [working from a story by him, David Giler and Walter Hill] picks up the thread 57 years later, when Sigourney Weaver and her cat (who have been in hibernation) are rescued by a deep space salvage team. The authorities ask her to accompany a team of marines back to the planet to investigate why all contact with the colony has suddenly been lost. Group sent this time consists of a bunch of tough grunts with a sour attitude about having been sent on such a dippy mission.

Weaver finds one human survivor – a cute, tough, terrified little girl played by Carrie Henn – on the planet.

The odds against the crew are, in a word, monstrous, and unsurprisingly, its members are dispatched one by one until it once again comes down to a battle royal between Weaver and one last monster.

Although film accomplishes everything it aims to do, overall impression is of a film made by an expert craftsman, while Scott clearly had something of an artist in him.

Weaver does a smashing job as Ripley. Carrie Henn is very appealing as the little girl and Jenette Goldstein makes a striking impression as a body-building recruit who is tougher than any of the guys in the outfit.

ALTERED STATES

1980, 102 mins, ◇ ⓥ *Dir* Ken Russell   US

★ *Stars* William Hurt, Blair Brown, Bob Balaban, Charles Haid

Altered States is an exciting combo science-fiction horror film. Direction by Ken Russell has energy to spare, with appropriate match-up of his baroque visual style to special effects intensive material.

Producers weathered stormy pre-production problems, including the ankling of director Arthur Penn late in 1978, departure soon after of special effects wiz John Dykstra, and

Veronica Cartwright, Tom Skerritt and John Hurt explore the alien spaceship in horror-sci-fi epic **Alien**.

transfer of project from Columbia to Warners as the proposed budget grew to $15 million. The plot's tall tale concerns a young psychophysiologist, Edward Jessup (played by William Hurt), who is working in New York and later at Harvard on dangerous experiments involving human consciousness.

Using himself as the subject, Jessup makes use of a sensory deprivation tank to hallucinate back to the event of his birth and beyond, regressing into primitive stages of human evolution.

Shattering use of Dolby stereo effects conspires with the images to give the viewer a vicarious LSD-type experience sans drugs. Hurt's feature film debut is arresting, especially during the grueling climactic sequence.

A

AMAZON WOMEN ON THE MOON

1987, 85 mins, ◇ ⓥ   *Dir* Joe Dante, Carl Gottlieb, Peter Horton, John Landis, Robert K. Weiss   US

★ *Stars* Rosanna Arquette, Ralph Bellamy, Carrie Fisher, Griffin Dunne, Steve Guttenberg, Russ Meyer

Amazon Women on the Moon is an irreverent, vulgar and silly film and has some hilarious moments and some real groaners too. John Landis & Co have found some 1980s things to satirize – like yuppies, the vidcassette biz, dating, condoms done up in a way that's not particularly shocking anymore.

Besides Landis, directors Joe Dante, Carl Gottlieb, Peter Horton and Robert K. Weiss take turns doing sketches – Weiss' *Amazon Women on the Moon* 1950s parody of bad sci-fi pics being the one that was stretched piecemeal throughout the film in a semi-successful attempt to hold this anthology together as one comedic work.

Eighteen other segs fill up the pic's 85 minutes, some mercifully short like Weiss' *Silly Pate* while Landis' *Hospital* is one of those slow-building, totally zany bits where the chuckles grow as the situation gets more ridiculous and you wish there was more.

ANDROID

1982, 80 mins, ◇ ⓥ   *Dir* Aaron Lipstadt   US

★ *Stars* Klaus Kinski, Brie Howard, Norbert Weisser, Crofton Hardester, Kendra Kirchner, Don Opper

Obsessed researcher Klaus Kinski inhabits a remote space station in the year 2036 with his android assistant, Max 404, played by co-writer Don Opper. Doctor is on the verge of perfecting his masterpiece, a perfect robot who happens to be a beautiful blonde, and who will render Max obsolete.

Onto the craft from a prison ship come three escaped convicts with no precise plans but with dangerous personalities. One way or another, they intend to make their way back to Earth, where a revolt by androids proved of sufficient magnitude to make them illegal.

Max wants to hitch a ride to the planet he's never seen, but Kinski's new creation and the rebellious renegades intervene with disruptive results.

Although there are the obligatory fight scenes and nudity, film works mainly due to the unusual interaction between the all-too-human Max robot and those around him.

Most pics of this ilk offer nothing but cardboard characters, so it's commendable that not only Max but the three fugitives come across with strong personalities. Kinski has relatively little to do, but is nevertheless plausible as a Dr Frankenstein type.

THE ANDROMEDA STRAIN

1971, 127 mins, ◇ ⓥ   *Dir* Robert Wise   US

★ *Stars* Arthur Hill, David Wayne, James Olson, Kate Reid, Paula Kelly, George Mitchell

The Andromeda Strain is a high-budget 'science-fact' melodrama, marked by superb production, an excellent score, an intriguing story premise and an exciting conclusion. But Nelson Gidding's adaptation of the Michael Crichton novel is too literal and talky.

In four acts representing days, a team of civilian medics attempt to find and isolate an unknown phenomenon which has killed most of a desert town near the place where a space satellite has fallen to earth. Arthur Hill, David Wayne, James Olson and Kate Reid are the specialists racing against time to determine why the town's only survivors are an old wino (George Mitchell) and an infant.

In the first half hour, the plot puzzle and eerie mood are well established, and in the final half hour there is a dramatically exciting climax with massive self-destruction machinery. The middle hour, however, drags proceedings numbingly. The four scientists repeatedly get into long-winded discussions. There are times when one wants to shout at the players to get on with it.

The glacial internal plot evolution is not at all relieved

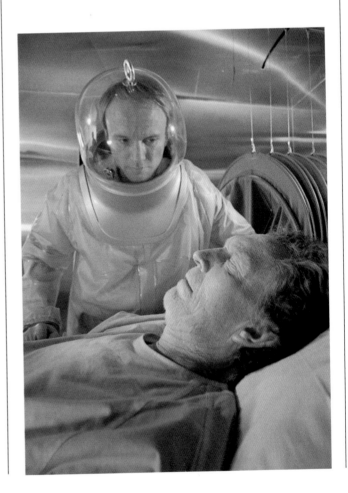

Scientist James Olson tries to fathom why wino George Mitchell survived **The Andromeda Strain.**

by the performances. Hill is dull; Wayne is dull; Olson caroms from another dull character to a petulant kid; and Reid's unexplained-until-later epilepsy condition does not generate much interest. Mitchell and nurse Paula Kelly are most refreshing changes of pace.

ATTACK OF THE 50 FT. WOMAN

1958, 65 mins, ⓥ *Dir* Nathan Hertz   US

★ *Stars* Allison Hayes, William Hudson, Yvette Vickers, Roy Gordon, George Douglas, Ken Terrell

Attack of the 50 Ft. Woman shapes up as a minor offering for the sci-fi trade where demands aren't too great.

The production is the story of a femme who overnight grows into a murderous giantess, out to get husband who's cheating with another woman. Growth was caused by ray burns suffered when she's seized by huge monster, who lands in the desert near home in a satellite from outer space. Breaking the chains used to restrain her in her luxurious mansion, she makes her way to a tavern where spouse is with his lady love and literally squeezes him to death before the sheriff kills her with a riot gun.

Allison Hayes takes title role as a mentally-disturbed woman who has been in a sanitarium, William Hudson is the husband and Yvette Vickers his girl friend, all good enough in their respective characters.

BACK TO THE FUTURE

1985, 116 mins, ◇ ⓥ *Dir* Robert Zemeckis   US

★ *Stars* Michael J. Fox, Christopher Lloyd, Crispin Glover, Lea Thompson, Claudia Wells, Thomas F. Wilson

The central winning elements in the scenario are twofold; hurtling the audience back to 1955, which allows for lots of comparative, pop culture humor, and delivering a 1985 teenager (Michael J. Fox) at the doorstep of his future parents when they were 17-year-old kids. That encounter is a delicious premise, especially when the young hero's mother-to-be develops the hots for her future son and his future father is a bumbling wimp.

Film is also sharply anchored by zestful byplay between Fox's Arthurian knight figure and Christopher Lloyd's Merlin-like, crazed scientist. The latter has mounted a nuclear-powered time machine in a spaced-out DeLorean car, which spirits the bedazed Fox 30 years back in time to the same little town in which he grew up.

In the film's opening sequences, the father (wonderfully played by Crispin Glover) is an unctuous nitwit, and the

mother (Lea Thompson) a plump, boozey, frau.

Performances by the earnest Fox, the lunatic Lloyd, the deceptively passionate Lea Thompson, and, particularly, the bumbling-to-confident Glover, who runs away with the picture, merrily keep the ship sailing.

BACK TO THE FUTURE PART II

1989, 107 mins, ◇ ⓥ *Dir* Robert Zemeckis   US

★ *Stars* Michael J. Fox, Christopher Lloyd, Lea Thompson, Thomas F. Wilson, Harry Waters Jr, Elizabeth Shue

The energy and heart which Robert Zemeckis and strong-writing partner Bob Gale (who takes solo screenplay credit this time) poured into the ingenious story of part one is diverted into narrative mechanics and camera wizardry in *Future II*.

The story starts exactly where the original left off, with Michael J. Fox's Marty McFly and Christopher Lloyd's visionary inventor Dr Emmett Brown taking off in their flying DeLorean time machine for 2015 on an urgent mission to save Fox's children from a terrible fate.

Future II finds the McFly family living in shabby lower-middle class digs in a world that isn't so much Orwellian as a gaudier and tackier projection of the present day.

What matters to Fox is that his son has become a wimp, just like his father was in the 1955 segment of the original film.

Then, in a curious narrative lapse, Fox picks up a sports almanac which, if taken back to the past, will enable him to get rich by gambling on future events. But villainous Biff (Thomas F. Wilson) absconds with it in the time machine to give it to his 1955 self, and the chase begins.

Zemeckis' fascination with having characters interact at different ages of their lives hurts the film visually, and strains credibility past the breaking point, by forcing him to rely on some very cheesy makeup designs.

BACK TO THE FUTURE PART III

1990, 118 mins, ◇ ⓥ *Dir* Robert Zemeckis   US

★ *Stars* Michael J. Fox, Christopher Lloyd, Mary Steenburgen, Thomas F. Wilson, Lea Thompson, Elisabeth Shue

Back to the Future Part III recovers the style and wit and grandiose fantasy elements in the original. The simplicity of plot, and the wide expansiveness of its use of space, are a refreshing change from the convoluted, visually cramped and cluttered second part.

Michael J. Fox's Marty McFly in his time-travelling DeLorean finds himself in the midst of a band of charging Indians in John Ford country, Monument Valley 1885. His mission is to bring back Doc (Christopher Lloyd) before he is shot in the back by Thomas F. Wilson's hilariously unhinged Buford 'Mad Dog' Tannen, an ancestor of McFly's 20th century nemesis Biff Tannen.

Fox steps into the background of the story and lets Lloyd have the chance to play the romantic lead for a change. Doc's offbeat romance with Mary Steenburgen's Clara Clayton, a spinster schoolmarm who shares his passion for Jules Verne, is funny, touching and exhilarating. Their ultimate journey through time gives the plot trajectory an unexpected and entirely satisfying resolution.

The fun of this meta-Western is partly the recognition of elements familiar from genre classics: the dance from *My Darling Clementine*, the sobering-up concoction from *El Dorado*, the costume from *Fistful of Dollars*. Fox re-experiences all this, literally flying through the screen (at an incongruous Monument Valley drive-in) into every Western fan's dream of being a character in a 'real' Western.

BARBARELLA

1968, 98 mins, ◇ Ⓥ   *Dir* Roger Vadim   FRANCE, ITALY

★ *Stars* Jane Fonda, John Phillip Law, Anita Pallenberg, Milo O'Shea, David Hemmings, Marcel Marceau

Despite a certain amount of production dash and polish and a few silly-funny lines of dialog, *Barbarella* isn't very much of a film. Based on what has been called an adult comic strip [by Jean Claude Forest], the Dino De Laurentiis production is flawed with a cast that is not particularly

adept at comedy, a flat script, and direction which can't get this beached whale afloat.

Jane Fonda stars in the title role, and comes across as an ice-cold, antiseptic, wide-eyed girl who just can't say no. Fonda's abilities are stretched to the breaking point along with her clothes.

In key supporting roles, John Phillip Law is inept as a simp angel while Anita Pallenberg, as the lesbian queen, fares better because of a well defined character.

Made at De Laurentiis' Rome studios, film can't really be called overproduced, considering the slapdash special effects, grainy process and poor calibre of the props, though put together on a massive scale so as to appear of spectacle proportions.

BATMAN

1966, 105 mins, ◇ ⊘   *Dir* Leslie H. Martinson   US

★ *Stars* Adam West, Burt Ward, Lee Merriwether, Cesar Romero, Burgess Meredith, Frank Gorshin

Batman is packed with action, clever sight gags, interesting complications and goes all out on bat with batmania: batplane, batboat, batcycle, etc. etc. Humor is stretched to the limit, color is comic-strip sharp and script retrieves every trick from the popular teleseries, adding a few more.

It's nearly impossible to attempt to relate plot. Suffice to say that it's Batman and Robin against his four arch-enemies, Catwoman, The Joker, The Penguin and The Riddler. Quartet have united and are out to take over the world. They elaborately plot the dynamic duo's death again and again but in every instance duo escape by the skin of their tights.

The acting is uniformly impressively improbable. The intense innocent enthusiasm of Cesar Romero, Burgess Meredith and Frank Gorshin as the three criminals is balanced against the innocent calm of Adam West and Burt Ward, Batman and Robin respectively.

BATMAN

1989, 126 mins, ◇ ⊘   *Dir* Tim Burton   US

★ *Stars* Michael Keaton, Jack Nicholson, Kim Basinger, Robert Wohl, Pat Hingle, Billy Dee Williams

Director Tim Burton effectively echoes the visual style of the original Bob Kane comics while conjuring up a nightmarish world of his own.

Going back to the source elements of the cartoon figure, who made his debut in 1939 for Detective (now DC) Comics, the Jon Peters-Peter Guber production will appeal to purists who prefer their heroes as straight as Clint Eastwood.

In a striking departure from his usual amiable comic-style, Michael Keaton captures the haunted intensity of the character, and seems particularly lonely and obsessive without Robin around to share his exploits.

The gorgeous Kim Basinger takes the sidekick's place, in a determined bow to heterosexuality which nonetheless leaves Batman something less than enthusiastic.

It comes as no surprise that Jack Nicholson steals every scene in a sizable role as the hideously disfigured Joker. Nicholson embellishes fascinatingly baroque designs with his twisted features, lavish verbal pirouettes and inspired excursions into the outer limits of psychosis. It's a masterpiece of sinister comic acting.

What keeps the film arresting is the visual stylization. It was a shrewd choice for Burton to emulate the jarring angles and creepy lighting of film noir.

The Doc (Christopher Lloyd) shows Marty McFly (Michael J. Fox)
his DeLorean time-travel machine in **Back to the Future.**

Left: *Jane Fonda as Barbarella, raygun-toting comic strip heroine of the Sixties sex-in-space epic.*

Above: *Michael Keaton's Batman confronts Jack Nicholson's The Joker in the adult-oriented vision of the Caped Crusader.*

BATTLE BEYOND THE STARS

1980, 104 mins, ◇ Ⓥ *Dir* Jimmy T. Murakami   US

★ *Stars* Richard Thomas, Robert Vaughn, George Peppard, John Saxon, Darlanne Fleugel, Sybil Danning

The fascination of watching how the defenseless cope with marauding barbarians is put to the test with New World's production of *Battle Beyond the Stars*.

In unfolding its saga of how the peace-loving bunch on a small planet rebuffs a genetically deficient but vicious band of bad guys, *Battle* incorporates touches of an old-fashioned western, horror pics and even a touch of softcore.

Despite the expense involved, the pic appears not to take itself too seriously. Principal characterizations are skin deep. Dialog takes the form of relaxed banter with a minimum of homilies.

George Peppard has fun as a Scotch-tippling cowboy from earth who turns up as one of the mercenaries hired by the planet's earnest young soldier (Richard Thomas). John Saxon is hilarious as the chief bad guy.

Below: *Space travel is merely the setting for a straight-forward actioner in* **Battle Beyond the Stars**.

B

Paul Williams and attendants in the final episode of the Apes saga, Battle for the Planet of the Apes.

BATTLE FOR THE PLANET OF THE APES

1973, 88 mins, ◇ ⓥ *Dir* J. Lee Thompson   US

★ *Stars* Roddy McDowall, Claude Akins, Natalie Trundy, Severn Darden, Lew Ayres, John Huston

The fifth and last film of the series depicts the confrontation between the apes and the nuclear mutated humans inhabiting a large city destroyed in previous episode. Roddy McDowall encores as the ape's leader, having his own tribal strife with Claude Akins, a militant trouble-maker.

Considering the usual fate of sequels, it's not so much that this final effort [from a story by Paul Dehn] is limp, but that the previous four pix maintained for so long a good quality level.

McDowell and Natalie Trundy head the cast, in which Paul Williams plays a philosopher-type, and Austin Soker is a black counselor, most respected of the humans who are more or less captives of the apes. Severn Darden is leader of

the mutated humans. Lew Ayres has a good bit, and John Huston appears in another pompous cameo as an aged philosopher of future generations who sets the flashback motif for the story.

BATTLETRUCK

1982, 91 mins, ◇ ⓥ *Dir* Harley Cokliss   US

★ *Stars* Michael Beck, Annie McEnroe, James Wainwright, John Ratzenberger, Randolph Powell, Bruno Lawrence

Battletruck is a well-made and engaging action picture. This is a feature debut for director Harley Cokliss, who was second-unit director of *The Empire Strikes Back.* Working on a limited budget in New Zealand, Cokliss gets more performing subtleties from his characters than these films usually have.

Pic takes place after civilization has nearly collapsed after the 'oil wars' depletes most of the world's petroleum supplies. The big truck is the main weapon for an outlaw army commandered by Straker (James Wainwright), excellent as a cold-blooded killer. However, his daughter Corlie (Annie McEnroe) doesn't share his ideas of a great career.

She flees and is befriended by reclusive biker Hunter (Michael Beck) and a peaceful community headed by Rusty (John Ratzenberger). From then on, it's a matter of counting the battles between Straker's band and Hunter's troops.

THE BEAST FROM 20,000 FATHOMS

1953, 80 mins, ⑰ *Dir* Eugene Lourie   US

★ **Stars** Paul Christian, Paula Raymond, Cecil Kellaway, Kenneth Tobey, Donald Woods, Lee Van Cleef

Producers have created a prehistoric monster that makes Kong seem like a chimpanzee. It's a gigantic amphibious beast that towers above some of New York's highest buildings. The sight of the beast stalking through Gotham's downtown streets is awesome. Special credit should go to Ray Harryhausen for the socko technical effects.

An experimental atomic blast in the Arctic region results in the 'unfreezing' of the strange prehistoric reptile of the dinosaur family. Scientist Tom Nesbitt's (Paul Christian)

report of the beast is attributed to hallucination resulting from Arctic exposure.

After several unsuccessful attempts, Nesbitt enlists the aid of Prof Thurgood Elson (Cecil Kellaway) and his pretty assistant Lee Hunter (Paula Raymond). Elson is killed by the monster while exploring an undersea canyon in a diving bell 150 miles from New York. The beast finally turns up in Manhattan.

Christian is first-rate as the determined scientist and Kellaway scores as the doubting professor. Raymond appears too stiff and unconvincing as the professor's assistant and Christian's romantic vis-a-vis. Screenplay [suggested by the *Saturday Evening Post* story *The Fog Horn* by Ray Bradbury] has a documentary flavor, which Jack Russell's camera captures expertly.

THE BEASTMASTER

1982, 118 mins, ◇ ⑰ *Dir* Don Coscarelli   US

★ **Stars** Marc Singer, Tanya Roberts, Rip Torn, John Amos, Josh Milrad, Rod Loomis

When *The Beastmaster* begins, it is very hard to tell what it is all about. An hour later, it is very hard to care what it is

The first of the monster-from-the-ice movies, The Beast from 20,000 Fathoms is still one of the best.

all about. Another hour later, it is very hard to remember what it was all about. From the early confusion, in which it seems that a cow gives birth to a baby boy, Marc Singer emerges as Dar.

Singer's destiny is to go after the villains led by Rip Torn to revenge the destruction of the village. Along the way he teams up with two ferrets, an eagle, a panther, Tanya Roberts and John Amos and other assorted creatures of equal acting ability. Much of the time they are involved in rescuing each other from rather noninteresting situations.

BEETLEJUICE

1988, 92 mins, ◇ Ⓥ *Dir* Tim Burton   US

★ **Stars** Alec Baldwin, Geena Davis, Michael Keaton, Catherine O'Hara, Glenn Shadix

Beetlejuice springs to life when the raucous and repulsive Betelgeuse (Michael Keaton) rises from his moribund state to wreak havoc on fellow spooks and mortal enemies.

Geena Davis and Alec Baldwin are a couple of affectionate New Englanders who live in a big barn of a house that they lovingly are restoring. But they crash over a covered bridge and drown – consigned to an afterlife that keeps them stuck at home forever invisible to anyone not similarly situated.

No sooner is their funeral over when their beloved house is sold to a rich New York financier (Jeffrey Jones) and his wife, the affected artiste (Catherine O'Hara). Help comes via a cryptically written book for the newly deceased that takes Davis and Baldwin into the afterlife – kind of a comical holding cell for people who died of unnatural causes like themselves – but better yet, from this freak of a character named Betelgeuse that lives in the graveyard that's part of the miniature table-top town that Baldwin built.

In the script [from a story by Michael McDowell and Larry Wilson], things above ground aren't nearly as inventive as they are below. Luckily, Keaton pops up from his grave to liven things up when the antics pitting the good ghosts against the intruders become a trite cat and mouse game.

BENEATH THE PLANET OF THE APES

1970, 95 mins, ◇ Ⓥ *Dir* Ted Post   US

★ **Stars** James Franciscus, Kim Hunter, Maurice Evans, Linda Harrison, Charlton Heston, Victor Buono

This sequel to the 1968 smash, *Planet of the Apes*, is hokey and slapdash – falling far short of the original.

Film utilizes closing sequence of the original – where Charlton Heston and the silent Linda Harrison ride into an unknown country on the supposedly unknown planet, only to find the head of the Statue of Liberty buried in the sand. Heston's curtain cry of anguish now is followed by new footage, as he and Harrison wander the vast wasteland, in which Heston suddenly disappears.

James Franciscus is yet another space explorer who crash-lands, centuries out of time. Dialog, acting and direction are substandard.

Heston appears in some new footage, and Franciscus actually looks just like a twin brother by this time, in face and in voice.

THE BLACK HOLE

1979, 97 mins, ◇ Ⓥ *Dir* Gary Nelson   US

★ **Stars** Maximilian Schell, Anthony Perkins, Robert Forster, Joseph Bottoms, Yvette Mimieux, Ernest Borgnine

The black hole itself gets short shrift in the screenplay, based on a story by Jeb Rosebrook, Bob Barbash and Richard Landau. Most of the pic is devoted to setting up the story of mad scientist Maximilian Schell, poised on the brink of his voyage to the unknown. An exploration ship staffed by Robert Forster, Anthony Perkins, Joseph Bottoms, Yvette Mimieux and Ernest Borgnine, stumbles on both Schell and the nearby black hole, with unpredictable results.

What ensues is sometimes talky but never dull. Director Gary Nelson's pacing and visual sense here are right on target.

In typical Disney fashion, the most attractive and sympathetic characters are not human at all. George F. McGinnis has constructed a bevy of robots that establish a mechanical world all their own.

BLADE RUNNER

1982, 114 mins, ◇ Ⓥ *Dir* Ridley Scott   US

★ **Stars** Harrison Ford, Rutger Hauer, Sean Young, Edward James Olmos, M. Emmet Walsh, Daryl Hannah

Ridley Scott's reported $30 million picture is a stylistically dazzling film noir set 37 years hence in a brilliantly imagined Los Angeles marked by both technological wonders and horrendous squalor.

Basic premise taken from a novel [*Do Androids Dream of Electric Sheep*] by Philip K. Dick provides a strong dramatic hook – replicants, robots designed to supply 'Off World' slave labor, are outlawed on earth. But a few of them have infiltrated LA, and retired enforcer Harrison Ford is recruited to eliminate them before they can do any damage.

One of them, beautiful Sean Young, is an advanced model with implanted memories so 'real' that even she doesn't know she's a replicant until she's tested by Ford.

Unfortunately, Young disappears for long stretches at a time, and at others Ford merely sits morosely around his apartment staring at photographs, which slows up the action.

Dramatically, film is virtually taken over at the midway point by top replicant Rutger Hauer. After destroying his creator, the massive, albino-looking Hauer takes off after Ford, and the villain here is so intriguing and charismatic that one almost comes to prefer him to the more stolid hero.

THE BLOB

1958, 85 mins, ◇ Ⓥ   *Dir* Irvin S. Yeaworth Jr   US

★ *Stars* Steve McQueen, Aneta Corseaut, Earl Rowe, Olin Howlin

The initial production of Jack H. Harris, a regional distrib in the Philadelphia area, *The Blob* had a reported budget of $240,000. Story, from an idea by Irvine H. Millgate, will tax the imagination of adult patrons.

A small Pennsylvania town has been plagued by teenage pranks. Hence, when highschoolers Steve McQueen and Aneta Corseaut report that a parasitic substance from outer space has eaten the local doctor and his nurse, no one will believe them. Especially when no bodies can be found.

Neither the acting nor direction is particularly creditable. McQueen, who's handed star billing, makes with the old college try while Corseaut also struggles valiantly as his girlfriend.

Star performers, however, are the camerawork of Thomas Spalding and Barton Sloane's special effects. Production values otherwise are geared to economy. Intriguing is the title number, written by Burt Bacharach and Mack David. It's sung offscreen by a harmony group as the credits unreel. The picture was lensed at the Valley Forge, Pa, studios.

Harrison Ford as replicant hunter Deckard high above the streets of L.A. **in Blade Runner.**

BRAINSTORM

1983, 106 mins, ◇ Ⓥ   *Dir* Douglas Trumbull   US

★ *Stars* Christopher Walken, Natalie Wood, Louise Fletcher, Cliff Robertson, Jordan Christopher, Joe Dorsey

Shaken and embattled during its completion phase, and carrying the memory of Natalie Wood's death *Brainstorm* is a high-tech $18 million movie dependent on the visualization of a fascinating idea.

Producer-director Douglas Trumbull's effects wizardry – and the concept behind it – is the movie. The fetching idea is a brain-wave device that gives characters the power to record and experience the physical, emotional and intellectual sensations of another human being.

On the downside, majority of players, including stars Christopher Walken and Wood as a married couple in a research environment, seem merely along for the ride. The film's acting surprise is Louise Fletcher, whose flinty, career scientist is a strong flavorful, workaholic portrait.

The film offers irrefutable evidence that Natalie Wood's drowning (in November 1981) did not cause the

Now something of a cult classic, low budget sic-fi pic **The Blob** *starred Steve McQueen (centre) and Aneta Corseaut.*

filmmakers to drastically re-write or re-shoot scenes. Her work appears intact and, reportedly, only one scene had to be changed (with actor Joe Dorsey replacing Wood in a scene with Walken).

Cliff Robertson earnestly plays the compromising head of a vast research complex that employs colleagues Walken and Fletcher. Predictably, a government bogeyman is trying to gum up pure science for the sake of national security.

BRAZIL

1985, 142 mins, ◇ Ⓥ   *Dir* Terry Gilliam   UK

★ *Stars* Jonathan Pryce, Robert De Niro, Michael Palin, Kim Greist, Katherine Helmond, Ian Holm

Brazil offers a chillingly hilarious vision of the near-future, set 'somewhere in the 20th Century.' Director Terry Gilliam reportedly wanted to call the film *1984½* As in Orwell's classic, society is monitored by an insidious, tentacular ministry, and the film's protagonist, a diligent but unambitious civil servant, Sam Lowry – played with vibrant comic imagination by Jonathan Pryce – becomes a victim of his own romantic delusions, and is crushed by a system he had never before thought of questioning.

He sees himself as a winged super-hero, part-Icarus, part-Siegfried, soaring lyrically through the clouds to the tune of 'Brazil', the old Xavier Cugat favorite, which as the film's ironic musical leitmotif, recurs in numerous mock variations.

Robert De Niro shows delightful comic flair in a small, but succulent characterization of a proletariat superhero, who disposes of some obnoxious rival repairmen in a disgustingly original manner, but meets a most bizarre end in the film's nightmare climax.

Gilliam has assembled a brilliant supporting cast of character actors, notably Ian Holm, as the edgy, paranoid ministry department chief hopelessly dependent on Pryce to untie bureaucratic knots.

BREWSTER MCCLOUD

1970, 104 mins, ◇ Ⓥ   *Dir* Robert Altman   US

★ *Stars* Bud Cort, Sally Kellerman, Michael Murphy, William Windom, Shelley Duvall, Rene Auberjonois

Brewster McCloud spares practically nothing in contemporary society. Literate original screenplay is a sardonic fairytale for the times, extremely well cast and directed.

Bud Cort heads the cast as a young boy, hiding in the depths of Houston's mammoth Astrodome where he is building wings. He is, or is not, in reality a bird in human form. His guardian angel is Sally Kellerman, always in the right spot to foil some nefarious person about to take advantage of Cort. Trouble is, her protection involves a series of unexplained murders.

Michael Murphy is the sleuth brought in from Frisco to help oldfashioned gumshoe G. Wood.

Kellerman gets sensational results from her part. She can project more ladylike sensuality and emotion in a look than most actresses can in an hour.

THE BROTHER FROM ANOTHER PLANET

1984, 104 mins, ◇ Ⓥ   *Dir* John Sayles   US

★ *Stars* Joe Morton, Darryl Edwards, Steve James, Leonard Jackson, Bill Cobbs, Maggie Renzi

John Sayles takes a turn toward offbeat fantasy in *The Brother from Another Planet*, a vastly amusing but progressively erratic look at the Harlem adventures of an alien, a black E.T.

Brother begins with a tall, mute, young black fellow seeming to be dumped unceremoniously in New York harbor. Within minutes, he makes his way to Harlem, where his unusual, but not truly bizarre, behavior raises some cackles but in most respects blends into the neighborhood.

Pic is essentially a series of behavioral vignettes, and many of them are genuinely delightful and inventive. Once the Brother discovers the Harlem drug scene, however, tale takes a rather unpleasant and, ultimately, confusing turn.

BUG

1975, 99 mins, ◇   *Dir* Jeannot Szwarc   US

★ *Stars* Bradford Dillman, Joanna Miles, Richard Gilliland, Jamie Smith Jackson, Alan Fudge, Jesse Vint

Bug concerns some mutated cockroaches liberated by an earthquake from the earth's core. Adapted from Thomas Page's book, *The Hephaestus Plague*, it starts off well with an earthquake in a farmland town, after which mysterious fires begin breaking out. The bugs, being from underground areas, are hot and eat carbon.

Bradford Dillman, an animal scientist, gets intrigued with them, so much so that, after wife Miles is incinerated in a bug attack, he becomes a recluse with the creatures and communicates with them. At the same time Dillman goes into seclusion, so does the film; its last half is largely static, and the film never revives much interest.

CAPRICORN ONE

1978, 127 mins, ◇ Ⓥ *Dir* Peter Hyams   US

★ *Stars* Elliott Gould, James Brolin, Brenda Vaccaro, Sam Waterston, O.J. Simpson, Hal Holbrook

Capricorn One begins with a workable, if cynical cinematic premise: the first manned space flight to Mars was a hoax and the American public was fooled through Hollywood gimmickry into believing that the phony landing happened.

Puppets of political intrigue, the earthbound astronauts of Capricorn One on a countdown to nowhere.

But after establishing the concept, Peter Hyams' script asks another audience – the one in the theatre – to accept something far more illogical, the uncovering of the hoax by reporter Elliott Gould.

The astronaut trio of James Brolin, Sam Waterston and O.J. Simpson together add up to nothing; there's no group chemistry. Still, scattershot casting means once in a while you hit and in the final scene Gould and Telly Savalas are teamed. The duo is a bullseye. Savalas, in a delightful cameo as a crop duster hired to help rescue Brolin in the desert and uncover the plot, is a marvelous complement to Gould.

Hal Holbrook plays the mission commander who calls off the Mars shot and engineers the dupe. His character must change from sincere – he believes he's doing the right thing by fooling the public – to menacing. In general, it is a script of conveniences.

CAT-WOMEN OF THE MOON

1953, 64 mins, Ⓥ *Dir* Arthur Hilton   US

★ *Stars* Sonny Tufts, Victor Jory, Marie Windsor, Carol Brewster, Susan Morrow, Bill Phipps

This imaginatively conceived and produced science-fiction yarn [an original story by producers Zimbalist and Rabin] takes the earth-to-moon premise and embellishes it with a civilization of cat-women on the moon.

Femmes, 2 million years ahead of Earth's civilization, very nearly wreck the earthmen's plans to return to their

home base, in a scheme to fly the rocket ship back to Earth themselves and eventually control this orbit. They use Marie Windsor, navigator on the flight, by making contact with her mentally before the constellation jaunt.

The cast ably portray their respective roles. Sonny Tufts is commander of the expedition, Victor Jory his co-pilot, and Bill Phipps and Doug Fowley are other members of party with Windsor. Carol Brewster is head of the cat-women, an enticing wench, and Susan Morrow also scores as a moon femme.

Arthur Hilton makes his direction count in catching the spirit of the theme, and art direction is far above average for a film of this calibre. William Whitley's 3-D photography provides the proper eerie quality.

CHERRY 2000

1988, 93 mins, ◇ Ⓥ *Dir* Steve de Jarnatt   US

★ **Stars** Melanie Griffith, David Andrews, Ben Johnson, Tim Thomerson, Harry Carey Jr, Pamela Gidley

A tongue-in-cheek sci-fi action pic which owes a considerable debt to the *Mad Max* movies, *Cherry 2000*'s greatest asset is top-billed Melanie Griffith, who lifts the material whenever she's on screen.

Griffith plays the part of E. Johnson, a tracker who lives at the edge of a desert known as The Zone. The year is 2017, and white-collar yuppie Sam Treatwell (David Andrews) seeks Johnson's help in replacing his beloved Cherry 2000 (Pamela Gidley), a robot sex-object who suffered internal meltdown when Treadwell unwisely tried to make love to her in soapsuds.

For obscure reasons, replacement Cherry clones are stored far out in the Zone, which is ruled over by the psychotic Lester (Tim Thomerson) and his gang. Bulk of the film [story by Lloyd Fonvielle] consists of efforts of Johnson and Treadwell to avoid capture by Lester and reach the robot warehouse.

Along the way they meet Ben Johnson who is a philosophical old-timer and Harry Carey Jr playing a treacherous gas-station owner.

Technically, pic is quite lavish and the Nevada locations suitably rugged.

CHILDREN OF THE DAMNED

1964, 90 mins, *Dir* Anton Leader   UK

★ **Stars** Ian Hendry, Alan Badel, Barbara Ferris, Alfred Burke, Sheila Allen, Clive Powell

Like most sequels *Children Of The Damned* isn't nearly as good as its predecessor – Metro's 1960 *Village of the Damned*. What weakens this sequel is the fact that, unlike the original, it is burdened with a 'message'.

Jack Briley's screenplay broadens the scope to an international scale of what was originally a taut little sci-fi

One of the **Children of the Damned** *challenges the might of present-day man in the British sci-fi thriller.*

shocker. This time those strange, handsome parthenogenetic children the genius IQs, destructive dispositions and raygun eyes are not mere invaders from the outer limits bent on occupying earth, but are actually premature samplings of man as he will be in, say, a million years. And they have arrived for a curious purpose – to be destroyed, presumably to enable the silly, warlike contemporary man to learn some sort of lesson.

There are one or two genuinely funny lines in Briley's scenario and they are inherited by the character of a geneticist played engagingly by Alan Badel. A few of Badel's scenes with Ian Hendry, who plays an idealistic psychologist, are the best in the picture. Otherwise it's tedious going, and Anton Leader's lethargic direction doesn't help any.

CITY LIMITS

1985, 85 mins, ◇ Ⓥ *Dir* Aaron Lipstadt   US

★ **Stars** Darrell Larson, John Stockwell, Kim Cattrall, Rae Dawn Chong, Robby Benson, James Earl Jones

Elements of *City Limits* fit it into the category of the post-holocaust pic, but the historical disaster is a plague which has wiped out an older generation. The young survive in a condition of controlled anarchy and resist attempts to impose a centralized government.

Most successful aspect of the film [based on a story by James Reigle and Aaron Lipstadt] is its depiction of a tribal lifestyle regulated according to rules learned from comic strips. Two gangs of bikers, the Clippers and the DAs, have divided up the city and live under a truce. Infractions of their pact are regulated with competitive jousting or acts of reciprocal revenge. The dead are cremated with their vehicles like Vikings in their boats. The two groups may unite against outside threats.

Less convincing is the portrayal, with allusions to Fritz Lang's classic *Metropolis*, of the totalitarian-inclined Sunya Corp., which attempts to take over the city with the initial cooperation of the DAs.

Film features an ace ensemble cast. Action scenes are well-executed and there's a vibrant score.

CLASH OF THE TITANS

1981, 118 mins, ◇ *Dir* Desmond Davis   UK

★ *Stars* Laurence Olivier, Harry Hamlin, Claire Bloom, Maggie Smith, Burgess Meredith, Ursula Andress

Clash of the Titans is an unbearable bore that will probably put to sleep the few adults stuck taking the kids to it. This mythical tale of Perseus, son of Zeus, and his quest for the 'fair' Andromeda, is mired in a slew of corny dialog and an endless array of flat, outdated special effects.

Watching acclaimed actors like Laurence Olivier, Maggie Smith and Claire Bloom wandering through the clouds in long white gowns as Greek gods is funny enough. But when they start to utter the stylized dialog about what they're going to do to the mortals on the earth below, one

Monster marathon: Clash of the Titans *was a feast for fans of Ray Harryhausen's special effects.*

wants to look to the Gods for help. But obviously, that's impossible here.

Unfortunately, none of the creatures of effects that famed expert Ray Harryhausen (who also co-produced) designed seem anything more than rehashes from B-pictures. Desmond Davids directs with a tired hand, not helped much by the lackadaisical writing.

CLASS OF 1999

1990, 98 mins, ◇ ⊘ *Dir* Mark L. Lester   US

★ *Stars* Bradley Gregg, Traci Lind, Malcolm McDowell, Stacy Keach, Pam Grier, John P. Ryan

A followup to the 1981 pic *Class of 84* this violent exploitation film is too pretentious for its own good. Director Mark L. Lester takes a cynical, fake-hip view of young people's future.

The inconsistent screenplay posits high-schoolers out of control. So-called free-fire zones have been set up in urban areas around the schools as no man's land, and are literally under the control of youth gangs.

Hamming it up as an albino megalomaniac, Stacy Keach is carrying out an experiment sending three androids reconverted from army surplus to serve as teachers at Kennedy H.S. in Seattle and whip the students into shape. Simultaneously, hero Bradley Gregg has been let out of jail

and returned to class at Kennedy in an experimental furlough program.

John P. Ryan and Pam Grier are loads of fun as the androids, latter mocking her image when not only her breasts but inner works are revealed for the final reel through hokey makeup effects.

CLOSE ENCOUNTERS OF THE THIRD KIND

1977, 135 mins, ◇ Ⓥ *Dir* Steven Spielberg   US

★ *Stars* Richard Dreyfuss, Francois Truffaut, Teri Garr, Melinda Dillon, Cary Guffey, Bob Balaban

Close Encounters of the Third Kind is a daring film concept which in its special and technical effects has been superbly realized. Steven Spielberg's film climaxes with a confrontation with life forms from another world.

Story involves a series of UFO appearances witnessed by Richard Dreyfuss, Indiana power company technician, and Melinda Dillon and her son Carey Guffey. Concurrent with this plot line are the maneuverings of a seemingly international and secret team of military and scientific personnel.

But there's no denying that the climax is an absolute stunner, literate in plotting, dazzling in execution and almost reverent in tone.

[In 1980 film was replaced by a 132-minute version, re-edited and with extra material. On posters, but not on prints, this was subtitled *The Special Edition*].

COCOON

1985, 117 mins, ◇ Ⓥ *Dir* Ron Howard   US

★ *Stars* Don Ameche, Wilford Brimley, Hume Cronyn, Brian Dennehy, Jack Gilford, Steve Guttenberg

A fountain of youth fable [from a novel by David Saperstein] which imaginatively melds galaxy fantasy with the lives of aging mortals in a Florida retirement home, *Cocoon* weaves a mesmerizing tale.

Film inventively taps a wellspring of universal desire: health and youth, a parable set, in this case, among a pallid group of denizens shuffleboarding their twilight days away until a mysterious quartet of normal-looking visitors shows up on their Floridian shores. They are arrivals from another galaxy, led by friendly Brian Dennehy and attractive Tahnee Welch (Raquel's daughter, in her first US film). Another nearly-silent member of the party is a debuting Tyrone Power Jr.

Dennehy hires a young, out-of-pocket charter boat skipper (engagingly played by Steve Guttenberg) for a plan to scuba dive for what appear to be weird, gigantic oyster shells. Dennehy rents an abandoned estate with a big indoor pool and rests the big pods in the pool's bottom.

Effectively intercut with these scenes is the life of the

The ultimate UFO movie, Close Encounters of the Third Kind set a new standard for the flying saucer saga.

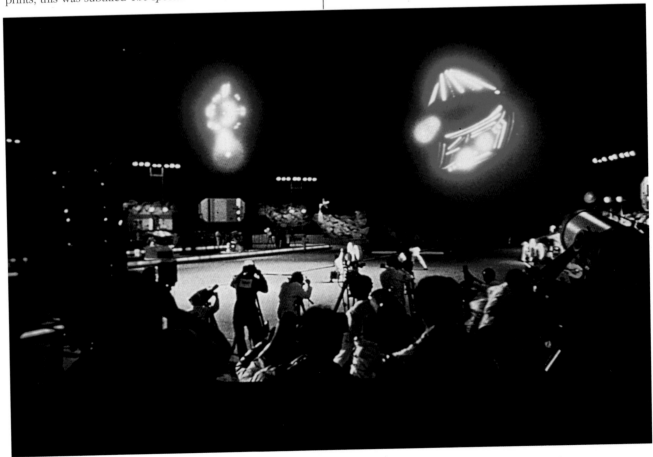

tight circle of nearby retirees, three of whom, played by Don Ameche, Wilford Brimley and Hume Cronyn, one day discover the cocoon-like shells and after a frolic in the water are soon diving in like 18-year-olds.

The effect of rejuvenation on the gray people, the inevitable mania when the whole retirement hospital wants in on the public bath, and the effect of this on the plans of the visitors from outer space propel the feature toward a suspenseful, ironic conclusion.

Senior citizen's sci-fi, Cocoon *and its sequel were modern-day evocations of the dream of an elixir of youth.*

COCOON: THE RETURN

1988, 116 mins, ◇ Ⓥ *Dir* Daniel Petrie   US

★ *Stars* Don Ameche, Wilford Brimley, Hume Cronyn, Steve Guttenberg, Maureen Stapleton, Jessica Tandy

Not altogether charmless, *Cocoon: The Return* still is far less enjoyable a senior folks' fantasy than *Cocoon.* An overdose of bathos weighs down the sprightliness of the characters, resulting in a more maudlin than magic effort.

Conquest of Space: based on a work of science-fact, The Mars Project, by rocket engineer Wernher von Braun.

Quandary begins with the return to St Petersburg, Fla, of the plucky group lead by the twinkle-eyed Don Ameche for a four-day visit from the utopian extra-terrestrial world of Antarea. Upon being reunited with family and friends, each questions his own choice for leaving in the first place and, at the end of the picture, the rationale for either returning to space or remaining on terra firma.

Jack Gilford as irascible widower Bernie Lefkowitz and Steve Guttenberg as Jack, the glass-bottom boat tour guide cum shlocky seashell merchandise salesman, keep this overly sappy production afloat.

Ameche, Gwen Verdon and occasionally Hume Cronyn want to play funny and loose but are restrained by Daniel Petrie's direction, which too often is unfocused.

THE COMPANY OF WOLVES

1984, 95 mins, ✧ Ⓥ *Dir* Neil Jordan   UK

★ *Stars* Angela Lansbury, David Warner, Stephen Rea, Tusse Silberg, Sarah Patterson, Graham Crowden

Admirably attempting an adult approach to traditional fairy tale material, *The Company of Wolves* nevertheless represents an uneasy marriage between old-fashioned storytelling and contemporary screen explicitness.

Virtually the entire film is the dream of the gravely beautiful adolescent Sarah Patterson. Within her dream are other dreams and stories told by others, all of which gives director Neil Jordan, who penned the screenplay with story originator Angela Carter, free imaginative rein, but which also gives the tale a less than propulsive narrative.

Anton Furst's elaborate forest settings, all created within studio-confines, are lovely. Jordan maneuvers well within them, even if Bryan Loftus' lush lensing is sometimes so dark that a claustrophobic feeling sets in.

CONQUEST OF SPACE

1955, 80 mins, ✧ *Dir* Byron Haskin   US

★ *Stars* Walter Brooke, Eric Fleming, Mickey Shaughnessy, Phil Foster, William Redfield, William Hopper

As in most science-fiction features of this type, it's the technical stuff, such as models, special photographic effects and process lensing that scores the best.

Here these assets support a rather stodgily developed screenplay [based on the book by Chesley Bonnestell and Willy Ley] and an unknown cast, both of which handicap the George Pall production putting its best foot forward.

The plot time of *Conquest of Space* is the future, with the setting divided between a space station wheeling some 1,000 miles above earth and a flight from this base to the planet Mars. The latter is a sort of red dust affair, sere and forbidding, and from which those who have survived are able to blast off for the return trip after some curiously unexciting adventures.

CONQUEST OF THE PLANET OF THE APES

1972, 87 mins, ◇ Ⓥ *Dir* J. Lee Thompson   US

★ *Stars* Roddy McDowall, Don Murray, Ricardo Montalban, Natalie Trundy, Hari Rhodes, Severn Darden

The *Planet of the Apes* series takes an angry turn in the fourth entry, *Conquest of the Planet of the Apes*.

The story begins about 20 years in the future, after a world epidemic has destroyed all dogs. People first had turned to apes as pets, but because of their intelligence the apes have become servants under civil regulation of computer-age overseer Don Murray. Into this milieu comes traveling circus operator Ricardo Montalban who, at the end of the prior film, had concealed the nearly-human offspring of the murdered Roddy McDowall and Kim Hunter. McDowall now has shifted to the role of his son.

In the new world, McDowall has to Uncle-Tom his way through the prevailing slave environment, until Murray's inexorable search for the long-missing ape-human child leads to Montalban's death under torture-grilling by Severn Darden. McDowall then organizes a bloody revolt which occupies the last third of the film.

COUNTDOWN

1968, 101 mins, ◇ Ⓥ *Dir* Robert Altman   US

★ *Stars* James Caan, Joanna Moore, Robert Duvall, Barbara Baxley, Charles Aidman, Steve Ihnat

Countdown, a story about a US space shot to the moon, is a literate and generally excellent programmer. Strong script [based on a novel by Hank Searls], emphasizing human conflict, is well developed and neatly resolved on a note of suspense.

James Caan is a civilian scientist, chosen because of political implications, to replace military officer Robert Duvall as the moon-shot man. Added to this conflict is that between Steve Ihnat, project boss, and Charles Aidman, flight surgeon, who carry on the struggle between safety of life considerations and those of beating the Russians.

Although the emphasis is on personal interactions, pic interpolates some stock footage plus specially-shot technical mock-up scenes.

CRACK IN THE WORLD

1965, 96 mins, ◇ *Dir* Andrew Marton   US

★ *Stars* Dana Andrews, Janette Scott, Kieron Moore, Alexander Knox, Peter Damon, Gary Lasdun

Crack in the World, distinguished principally by some startling special effects, imaginatively focuses on an ill-fated experiment to tap the unlimited energy residing within the earth's core which nearly blows up the world.

Produced in Spain for Philip Yordan's Security Pictures, the Paramount release carries a more legitimate premise than the regular science-fiction entry, strictly fictional in tone and context. Here is an entirely logical scientific operation, of drilling through the earth's crust to reach the molten mass called magma, which, brought to the surface under controlled conditions, could give the world all the energy it would ever want.

Dana Andrews plays part of the scientist in charge of the operation, dying with fast cancer, and Kieron Moore his assistant who believes his superior's plan will end in the disaster which eventuates, both handling their roles okay. Janette Scott is Andrews' scientist-wife, actually in love with Moore, a rather thankless role which she sparks as much as possible.

CRIMES OF THE FUTURE

1970, 63 mins, ◇ *Dir* David Cronenberg   CANADA

★ *Stars* Ronald Mlodzik, Jon Lidolt, Tania Zolty, Paul Mulholland, Jack Messinger, Iain Ewing

Made on a $20,000 budget, David Cronenberg's second feature film, *Crimes of the Future*, bears a strong similarity to his first outing, *Stereo*, produced the year before.

Cronenberg's obsession for such matters as bodily mutation and grotesque growths, aberrant medical experiments, massive plagues and futuristic architecture are all here in a convoluted look at a future gone perverse.

The world's entire female population has evidently been wiped out, and the male population has turned to various, and disappointingly tame, alternative sexual fixations. Prime symptom of the illness is Rouge's Foam, a substance which leaks from bodily orifices and is sexually exciting in its initial stage, but deadly later on.

As he moves through the bleak but architecturally striking settings, the main character Tripod begins to take on the dimensions of an Edgar Allan Poe hero, a doomed figure traversing a devastated landscape.

DALEKS INVASION EARTH 2150 A.D.

1966, 84 mins, ◇ Ⓥ *Dir* Gordon Flemying   UK

★ *Stars* Peter Cushing, Bernard Cribbins, Ray Brooks, Andrew Keir, Roberta Tovey, Jill Curzon

Dr Who, in his time and space machine, arrives in London in A.D. 2150 to find it ravaged after a Dalek invasion. The

Peter Cushing as Dr Who, with Bernard Cribbins and Roberta Tovey, in **Daleks Invasion Earth 2150 A.D.**

earth's cities have been razed by meteorites and cosmic rays and human beings have been turned into living dead men called Robomen. Prisoners have been taken and forced to work in a secret mine as slaves.

It is all fairly naive stuff decked out with impressive scientific jargon. Peter Cushing, as the professor; Jill Curzon, as his niece, and Roberta Tovey, as the granddaughter, have learned to play it with the necessary seriousness. Bernard Cribbins as the policeman provides some amusing light relief.

DAMNATION ALLEY

1977, 95 mins, ◇ 🆅 *Dir* Jack Smight   US

★ *Stars* Jan-Michael Vincent, George Peppard, Dominique Sanda, Paul Winfield, Jackie Earle Haley, Kip Niven

Damnation Alley is dull, stirred only occasionally by prods of special effects that only seem exciting compared to the dreariness that proceeded it. What's worse, it's dumb, depending on its stereotyped characters to do the most stupid things under the circumstances in order to keep the story moving.

Jan-Michael Vincent and George Peppard are air force officers on duty in a desert missile bunker when World War

III comes with a lot of stock shots of mushroom explosions.

Skip forward a couple of years through titled explanations that most of the country was destroyed and Earth tilted on its axis. But Vincent and Peppard are still in the desert with the other troops.

THE DAMNED

1963, 87 mins, *Dir* Joseph Losey   UK

★ *Stars* Macdonald Carey, Shirley Anne Field, Viveca Lindfors, Alexander Knox, Oliver Reed, Walter Gotell

'What is a director's picture?' This one is. Although the cast is excellent, no one character dominates the action or overshadows the others. Joseph Losey's hand is so apparent that the film's considerable effectiveness must be accredited to him as must its few faults and the fearsome message it conveys.

Much of the film's appeal is visual, although the dialog is a credit to the scripter Evan Jones, [from H.L. Lawrence's novel *The Children of Light*. The only objection is in its failure to take a stand.

Macdonald Carey, Shirley Anne Field, Alexander Knox (particularly good), Viveca Lindfors and Oliver Reed have principal roles in the quasi-sci-fi story which centers on a group of children being exposed to radiation in preparation for the day predicted by Knox when global nuclear warfare will destroy all living things – except these few.

All the principals are excellent, with Reed playing a Teddy boy and brother of Field although his interest in her is strongly incestuous.

THE DARK CRYSTAL

1983, 94 mins, ◇ ⓥ *Dir* Jim Henson, Frank Oz   UK

The Dark Crystal, besides being a dazzling technological and artistic achievement by a band of very talented artists and performers, presents a dark side of *Muppet* creators Jim Henson and Frank Oz that could teach a lesson in morality to youngsters at the same time as it is entertaining their parents.

While there is plenty of humor in the film, it is actually an allegory of the triumph of good over evil, of innocence over the wicked. This world is inhabited with monstrously evil Skeksis, who are temporarily in command of the world wherein only a handful of wise and virtuous creatures manage to stay alive.

Until, of course, Jen and Kira, a boy and girl gelfling, set out to defeat the Skeksis by replacing a shard that has been taken from the Dark Crystal, which awaits its return before Doomsday is due.

The creation of a small world of memorable characters is the main contribution of Henson and Oz. The outstanding character is the Aughra, an ancient one-eyed harridan of an oracle who somehow manages to remind one of a truly blowsy Shelley Winters.

DARK STAR

1974, 83 mins, ◇ ⓥ *Dir* John Carpenter   US

★ **Stars** Brian Narelle, Andreijah Pahich, Carl Duniholm, Dan O'Bannon

Dark Star is a limp parody of Stanley Kubrick's *2001: A Space Odyssey* that warrants attention only for some remarkably believable special effects achieved with very little money. [Pic began in 1970 as 45-minute USC Film School short. Final budget was $60,000.]

The screenplay cloisters four astronauts together on a lengthy extraterrestrial jaunt. To pass the time, the men joke, record their diaries on videotape, take sunlamp treatments, reminisce about their past earth lives and play with their alien mascot (an inflated beach ball with claws). Eventually their talking female computer misfires, the spaceship conks out and only one, an ex-surfer, manages to career back to earth on an improvised board.

The dim comedy consists of sophomoric notations and mistimed one-liners.

D.A.R.Y.L.

1985, 99 mins, ◇ ⓥ *Dir* Simon Wincer   US

★ **Stars** Mary Beth Hurt, Michael McKean, Kathryn Walker, Colleen Camp, Josef Sommer, Ron Frazier

D.A.R.Y.L. manages to get off to a strong start with a scenic chase through a curving mountain road as a chopper bears down on a racing car. Just before crashing, the driver pushes out a young boy who is rescued and then taken into a foster home by the Richardsons (Mary Beth Hurt and Michael McKean). The Richardsons later find that this strange young man is a robot.

After establishing a cozy domestic situation the film takes off in a different direction when his 'parents' come to take Daryl home. Home is a top security research facility where scientists Josef Sommer and Kathryn Walker have given birth to D.A.R.Y.L. Acronym stands for Data Analyzing Robot Youth Lifeform and Daryl is described as 'an experiment in artificial intelligence.'

Second half of the picture is the most farfetched and also the most fun as the young robot gets to show off some of his powers.

THE DAY OF THE TRIFFIDS

1963, 93 mins, ◇ ⓥ *Dir* Steve Sekely   UK

★ **Stars** Howard Keel, Kieron Moore, Janette Scott, Nicole Maurey, Mervyn Johns

Basically, this is a vegetarian's version of *The Birds*, a science-fiction-horror melodrama about a vile people-eater of the plant kingdom with a voracious appetite. Although riddled with script inconsistencies and irregularities, it is a more-than-adequate film of its genre.

John Wyndham's novel served as the source for exec producer Philip Yordan's screenplay. The proceedings begin with a spectacular display of celestial fireworks, a meteorite shower that leaves the earth's population heir to two maladies: blindness and the sinister company of a fast- multiplying plant aptly called Triffidus Celestus that looks like a Walt Disney nightmare and sounds like a cauldron of broccoli cooking in Margaret Hamilton's witchin' kitchen.

Hero of the piece is Howard Keel as a Yank seaman who, ironically spared the ordeal of blindness by having had his ill optics bandaged during the meteorite invasion, makes his way through a world haplessly engaged in a universal game of blind man's buff while under mortal threat of the carnivorous chlorophyll. Ultimately a marine biologist (Kieron Moore) stranded in a lighthouse with his wife (Janette Scott) discovers the means to dissolve and destroy the triffid.

The acting is generally capable. Steve Sekely's other-

Above: *Muppeteers Jim Henson and Frank Oz's fantasy* The Dark Crystal *is a visually-stunning modern morality tale.*

Below: *Space satire on a shoe-string budget,* Dark Star *has achieved cult status as an interstellar black comedy.*

SCIENCE-FICTION MOVIES

ously might save the grave situation and the world's powers unite, for once, to help a possibly doomed civilization.

Drama of this situation is played out as a newspaper scoop. Picture was shot largely in the building of the *Daily Express*. Arthur Christiansen, ex-editor of the *Express*, acted as technical advisor as well as playing the editor.

Guest's direction is brisk and makes good use of newsreel sequences and special effects, designed by Les Bowie. Dialog is racy and slick without being too parochial for the layman.

The acting all round is effective. Edward Judd, making his first star appearance, clicks as the hero, the reporter who brings in the vital facts that make the story take shape. He shows rugged charm in his lightly romantic scenes with Janet Munro, who is pert and pleasant in the only considerable distaff role. Outstanding performance comes from Leo McKern, who is tops as a dependable gruff and understanding science reporter.

THE DAY THE EARTH STOOD STILL

1951, 92 mins, Ⓥ *Dir* Robert Wise   US

★ *Stars* Michael Rennie, Patricia Neal, Hugh Marlowe, Sam Jaffe, Billy Gray

Screenplay, based on a story by Harry Bates, tells of an invasion of the earth by a single spaceship from an unidentified planet in outer space. Ship has two occupants, an eight-foot robot, and an earth-like human. They have come to warn the earth's people that all other inhabited planets have banded together into a peaceful organization and that peace is being threatened by the wars of the earth-people. If that happens, the inter-planetary UN is prepared to blast the earth out of the universe.

Spaceship lands in Washington and the man, leaving the robot on guard, leaves to hide among the people, to discover for himself what they are like. His findings of constant bickerings and mistrust aren't too favorable for the earth's humans. Situation naturally creates fear throughout the world and the US brings out army tanks, howitzers, etc, to guard the ship and the robot, while a frantic search goes on for the man.

Cast, although secondary to the story, works well. Michael Rennie is fine as the man from space. Patricia Neal is attractive and competent as the widowed mother of the young boy whom he befriends and who is the first to know his secret.

wise able direction has a bothersome flaw in the contradictory manner in which the triffids seem to approach and assault their victims.

THE DAY THE EARTH CAUGHT FIRE

1961, 99 mins, Ⓥ *Dir* Val Guest   UK

★ *Stars* Janet Munro, Leo McKern, Edward Judd, Bernard Braden, Michael Goodliffe, Peter Butterworth

Val Guest's production has a fascinating yarn, some very sound thesping and an authentic Fleet Street (newspaper) background.

By mischance, an American nuclear test at the South Pole is conducted on the same day as a Russian one at the North Pole. It first causes a sinister upheaval in the world's weather and then it is discovered that the globe has been jolted out of orbit and is racing towards the sun and annihilation. It's figured that four giant bombs exploded simultane-

DEATH RACE 2000

1975, 78 mins, ◇ *Dir* Paul Bartel   US

★ *Stars* David Carradine, Simone Griffeth, Sylvester Stallone, Mary Woronov, Roberta Collins, Martin Kove

Roger Corman's quickie production deals with ultra-violent sport in a futuristic society, in this case an annual cross-country road race with drivers scoring points by running down pedestrians.

Script, from an Ib Melchior story, makes its satirical points economically, and director Paul Bartel keeps the film moving quickly. Almost all of the film takes place on the road, with carnage and crashes occurring like clockwork. David Carradine, clad in a spooky black leather outfit, is the national champion driver, challenged by thug-like Sylvester Stallone and four other drivers, including Amazon-like Mary Woronov. While fending off Stallone's attacks, Carradine also has to deal with radicals trying to sabotage the race.

DEATHSPORT

1978, 83 mins, ◇ ⑰ *Dir* Henry Suso, Allen Arkush   US

★ *Stars* David Carradine, Claudia Jennings, Richard Lynch, William Smithers, Will Walker, David McLean

Deathsport is Roger Corman's futuristic science-fiction gladiator picture. And what is a futuristic science-fiction gladiator picture? It's a film set 1,000 years into the future, post neutron wars, where the good warriors ride horses and wield see-through sabres fighting bad guys known as Statesmen who drive lethal motorcycles known as 'Death Machines'.

The good guys, Ranger Guides, are quiet, live by a code, make temporary unions and roam desert wastelands trying to avoid the cannibal mutants and those motorcycles, which are very noisy.

Statesmen have other plans. They have two ways of amusing themselves: beating up Ranger Guides – no easy task since Ranger Guides are superior warriors – and capturing female rangers, who they strip, lock up in dark room with metal chandeliers and then apply electricity and special effects. Nice guys.

David Carradine is the quiet good guy and the best thing that can be said about his acting and his part is that he doesn't say much. Claudia Jennings is his partner good guy, the one who gets to amuse the bad guy in the dark room. The best thing that can be said about her performance is that she gets to take off her clothes, twice.

DEATHWATCH

1980, 128 mins, ◇ ⑰ *Dir* Bertrand Tavernier   FRANCE, W. GERMANY

★ *Stars* Romy Schneider, Harvey Keitel, Harry Dean Stanton, Therese Liotard, Max Von Sydow

The story, shrewdly crafted by Bertrand Tavernier and American screenwriter David Rayfiel from a novel by David Compton [*The Unsleeping Eye*], is a throat-catcher. In a future society people die of old-age, science having almost completely banished disease.

A cunning TV producer, Vincent Ferriman, played with chillingly unctuous serenity by Harry Dean Stanton, hits upon the idea of a TV program that would cover live the last days of an individual who has managed to contract a terminal illness.

Ferriman's proposed subject is Katherine Mortenhoe (finely played by Romy Schneider), whose fierce independence and sensitivity would seem to provide poignant fodder for the camera eye. But Katherine, after signing a contract, flees the city.

Deathwatch is a compelling drama centered on the human implications of its fanciful premise, as well as a harsh indictment of the media's role in society.

DEEPSTAR SIX

1989, 100 mins, ◇ ⑰ *Dir* Sean S. Cunningham   US

★ *Stars* Taurean Blacque, Nancy Everhard, Greg Evigan, Miguel Ferrer, Nia Peeples, Cindy Pickett

Director-producer Sean Cunningham molds this tale of a sea monster attacking an ocean-bottom research team [story by Lewis Abernathy].

Crew, while trying to create a level launch site for some ocean-floor navy missiles, blows up a cavern in which the creature has been dwelling for eons. Enraged, it attacks their craft, manages to get inside, and more or less picks them off one by one.

But effect is diluted by implausibility, as creature never seems real – more like a goof on a 1950s horror movie monster than a true threat.

Pic's cast is a grab-bag ensemble with no real center (toplined Taurean Blacque is killed early on). It eventually finds its emotional core in an affair between crewmen Greg Evigan and Nancy Everhard. A sharp performance by Miguel Ferrer as a punchy, smartmouthed crewmen is diluted when character goes campily berserk.

DEMON SEED

1977, 94 mins, ◇ ⑰ *Dir* Donald Cammell   US

★ *Stars* Julie Christie, Fritz Weaver, Gerrit Graham, Berry Kroeger, Lisa Lu, Larry J. Blake

Demon Seed tells of the impregnation of a female by a master computer system which seeks to perpetuate itself in human form. Julie Christie stars as the electronic Eve, along with Fritz Weaver as her scientist husband.

Excellent performances and direction (Donald Cammell), from a most credible and literate screenplay [from a novel by Dean R. Koontz], make production an intriguing achievement in story-telling.

Christie and Weaver live adjacent to an advanced computer center. Their marriage is crumbling because of his commitment to a new machine, Proteus IV, designed to do almost everything but think.

The burden of the story falls on Christie and she does indeed make the film come off.

DRAGONSLAYER

1981, 108 mins, ◇ Ⓥ *Dir* Matthew Robbins UK

★ *Stars* Peter MacNicol, Caitlin Clarke, Ralph Richardson, John Hallam, Peter Eyre, Chloe Salaman

A well-intentioned fantasy with some wonderful special effects, *Dragonslayer* falls somewhat short on continuously intriguing adventure. Technically speaking, it is an expertly mounted period piece concerning a boy's attempt to slay a fire-breathing dragon in order to save an entire kingdom. However, the story line is often tedious and the major action sequences appear much too late in the picture.

Ralph Richardson limns the properly mysterious (and too seldom seen) sorcerer that members of a neighbouring kingdom seek as the only person who can slay the terrorizing dragon.

Early on Richardson's powers are put to the test by a representative of the king, who seems to kill the sorcerer. It is then up to his apprentice, newcomer Peter MacNicol, to fight the dragon with the magic at his disposal.

MacNicol has the proper look of innocence to be a little unnatural in his performance. Along the way he is given nice support by Caitlin Clarke as a spunky love interest.

The real stars (as expected) of this film are the fabulous special effects. Given the high failure rate, it's especially refreshing to see experts come up with the imaginative and effective devices.

DR. CYCLOPS

1940, 75 mins, ◇ Ⓥ *Dir* Ernest Schoedsack US

★ *Stars* Albert Dekker, Janice Logan, Thomas Coley, Charles Halton, Victor Kilian, Frank Yaconelli

In detailing the discoveries of a madman scientist wherein he is able to reduce the size of men and animals to miniature pygmies, story and direction both fail to catch and hold interest. Achieved through continual use of process and trick photography, idea gets lost in a jumble and pancakes off for a dull effort.

Albert Dekker, researching in the jungles of South America, finds a rich radium deposit from which he can draw concentrated energy for experimental use. He has already used the power to reduce animals to minute size, when a pair of mining engineers (Thomas Coley and Victor Kilian) and two biologists (Janice Logan and Charles Halton) arrive and soon discover his secret. Dekker gets the quartet, together with native Frank Yaconelli, into the radium machine room and reduces the group down to beings of a foot tall. From there on, it's an unexciting adventure to escape the madman; which early expectation of him dropping into his bottomless well finally culminating.

As effects of radium treatment wears off, the human guinea pigs gradually return to normal size for return to the outside world.

DREAMSCAPE

1984, 95 mins, ◇ Ⓥ *Dir* Joe Ruben US

★ *Stars* Dennis Quaid, Max Von Sydow, Christopher Plummer, Eddie Albert, Kate Capshaw, David Patrick Kelly

Film centers on 'dreamlinking', the psychic projection of one person's consciousness into a sleeping person's subconscious, or his dreams. If that sounds far-fetched, it is. Central character is played with gusto by Dennis Quaid as Alex Garland, a reluctant ex-psychic who hooks up with Dr Paul Novotny (Max Von Sydow), who runs a dream research project at the local college that has an elaborate laboratory setup to study the phenomena.

There he meets Dr Jane de Vries (Kate Capshaw), Von Sydow's chief assistant who secretly lusts after Quaid, but only until he 'eavesdrops' on her erotic dream that involves Quaid. Enter Christopher Plummer as Bob Blair, a secretive and despicable government type who finances and oversees Von Sydow's research, but covertly plans to use its results for sinister ends.

DR. STRANGELOVE OR: HOW I LEARNED TO STOP WORRYING AND LOVE THE BOMB

1964, 102 mins, Ⓥ *Dir* Stanley Kubrick UK

★ *Stars* Peter Sellers, George C. Scott, Sterling Hayden, Keenan Wynn, Slim Pickens, James Earl Jones

Academy Award 1964: Best Picture (Nomination)

Nothing would seem to be farther apart than nuclear war and comedy, yet Kubrick's caper eloquently tackles a *Fail Safe* subject with a light touch.

Screenplay based on the book *Red Alert* by Peter George is imaginative and contains many an offbeat touch. Some of the characters have a broad brush in their depiction, but this is the very nature of satire.

It all begins when a Strategic Air Command general on his own initiative orders bomb-carrying planes under his command to attack Russia. From here on it's a hectic, exciting series of events, alternating between the General who has started it all, the planes en route to the USSR, and the Pentagon's war room, where the Chief Executive is trying his best to head off the nuclear war.

It would seem no setting for comedy or satire, but the writers have accomplished this with biting, piercing dialogue and thorough characterizations. Peter Sellers is excellent, essaying a trio of roles – a British RAF captain assigned to the US base where it all begins, the President and the title character, Dr Strangelove, a German scientist aiding the US whose Nazi mannerisms overcome him.

George C. Scott as the fiery Pentagon general who

Variety

D U N E

© 1983, 1984 Universal City Studios, Inc.

Printed in England

seizes on the crisis as a means to argue for total annihilation of Russia offers a top performance, one of the best in the film. Odd as it may seem in this backdrop, he displays a fine comedy touch. Sterling Hayden is grimly realistic as the General who takes it on his own to send our nuclear bomb-carrying planes to attack Russia. He is a man who blames the Communists for fluoridation of water, and just about everything else.

DR. WHO & THE DALEKS

1965, 83 mins, ◇ ⓥ *Dir* Gordon Flemyng   UK

★ *Stars* Peter Cushing, Roy Castle, Jennie Linden, Roberta Tovey, Barrie Ingham, Geoffrey Toone

Absentminded professor Dr Who (Peter Cushing) has invented Tardis, a Time and Relative Dimension in Space Machine, capable of lugging people to other worlds, in other eras. By accident, the prof, his granddaughters (Jennie Linden and Roberta Tovey) and Linden's boyfriend (Roy Castle) are ejected from the earth and land on a huge, petrified planet at a time many years back. The planet is ravaged with radiation from a previous war and the quartet

Kyle MacLachlan (left) with Sting (right), duelling it out in David Lynch's vision of the Sixties best-seller Dune.

finds themselves in a struggle between the Daleks and the Thals. The Daleks, protected from radiation in an all-metal city and wearing mobile metal cones fitted with flame-guns, are determined to wipe out the gentle Thals.

Cushing plays Dr Who with amiable gravity. Linden is a pretty, routine heroine while Tovey is pleasantly cast as the little girl with scientific knowhow and commonsense. Roy Castle mugs and falls around a little too zestfully as the boyfriend with a fairly good sense of humor.

DUNE

1984, 140 mins, ◇ ⓥ *Dir* David Lynch   US

★ *Stars* Francesca Annis, Brad Dourif, Kyle MacLachlan, Sian Phillips, Sting, Max Von Sydow

Dune is a huge, hollow, imaginative and cold sci-fi epic. Visually unique and teeming with incident, David Lynch's film holds the interest due to its abundant surface attractions but won't, of its own accord, create the sort of fanaticism which has made Frank Herbert's 1965 novel one of the all-time favorites in its genre.

Set in the year 10,991, *Dune* is the story of the coming to power of a warrior savior and how he leads the lowly inhabitants of the Dune planet to victory over an evil emperor and his minions.

Lynch's adaptation covers the entire span of the novel, but simply setting up the various worlds, characters, intrigues and forces at work requires more than a half-hour of expository screen time.

The anointed one, Paul Atreides, travels with his regal mother and father to the desert planet, where an all-powerful 'spice' is mined from beneath the sands despite the menace provided by enormous worms which gobble up harvesters in a single gulp.

The horrid Harkonnens conquer the city on Dune, but Paul and his mother escape to the desert. There Paul trains native warriors and achieves his full mystic powers.

Francesca Annis and Jurgen Prochnow make an outstandingly attractive royal couple, Sian Phillips has some mesmerizing moments as a powerful witch, Brad Dourif is effectively loony, and best of all is Kenneth McMillan, whose face is covered with grotesque growths and who floats around like the Blue Meanie come to life.

EDWARD SCISSORHANDS

1990, 98 mins, ◇ ⓥ *Dir* Tim Burton   US

★ *Stars* Johnny Depp, Winona Ryder, Dianne Wiest, Anthony Michael Hall, Alan Arkin, Kathy Baker

Director Tim Burton takes a character as wildly unlikely as a boy whose arms end in pruning shears, and makes him the center of a delightful and delicate comic fable.

Johnny Depp plays Edward, who lives in isolation in a gloomy mansion on the hill until a sunny Avon lady (Dianne Wiest) discovers him and takes him into her suburbia home and mothers him like a crippled bird. The creation of an inventor (Vincent Price) who died and left him unfinished, Edward sports an astonishing pair of hands – five-fingered, footlong blades that render him either lethal or extraordinarily skilful.

For the bevy of bored housewives in the pastel-colored nabe, gentle and exotic Edward becomes an instant celeb who amuses them by artistically pruning their hedges, their dogs and their coiffures.

But when he's wrongly accused in a burglary, his star falls and they turn on him. Meanwhile his wistful and impossible attraction to Kim (Winona Ryder), the Avon lady's teenage daughter, adds another level of tension.

Depp, former TV teen idol in his second starring screen role, gives a sensitive reading of Edward. With Ryder

kept mostly in the background, Wiest's mother figure shares the screen with Depp, and she's a smash. Also a hoot is Alan Arkin as her unexcitable husband, and Kathy Baker as a sex-starved vixen.

EMBRYO

1976, 108 mins, ◇ ⓥ *Dir* Ralph Nelson   US

★ *Stars* Rock Hudson, Diane Ladd, Barbara Carrera, Roddy McDowall, Ann Schedeen, John Elerick

The story has doctor Rock Hudson grow a beautiful young woman (Barbara Carrera) in his laboratory from fetal beginnings. It's kind of a *Bride of Frankenstein* tale, cast in terms of scientific mumbo-jumbo, an effective blending of old and new plot elements.

Hudson plays with gentleness and restraint, and Carrera's pristine fashion-model beauty is perfect for the role, but there's little feeling of genuine passion or eroticism.

The script [from a story by Jack W. Thomas] is much stronger on plot than it is on character relationships. Suspense built up before Carrera's birth is dissipated in clumsy dramatic confrontations when she and Hudson set out in society.

Diane Ladd is certainly wasted here as Hudson's jealous housekeeper.

EMPIRE OF THE ANTS

1977, 89 mins, ◇ ⓥ *Dir* Bert I. Gordon   US

★ *Stars* Joan Collins, Robert Lansing, John David Carson, Albert Salmi, Jacqueline Scott, Pamela Shoop

The H.G. Wells-inspired exploitationer *Empire of the Ants*, is an above-average effort about ants that grow big after munching on radioactive waste, and then terrorize a group of people headed by Joan Collins, Robert Lansing and John David Carson.

Periodic moments of good special effects are separated by reels of dramatic banality as players flounder in flimsy dialog and under sluggish direction.

Collins is a sharpie Florida real estate agent who takes a group of potential suckers on Lansing's boat to remote swampland. There the big ants attack.

THE EMPIRE STRIKES BACK

1980, 124 mins, ◇ ⓥ *Dir* Irvin Kershner   US

★ *Stars* Mark Hamill, Harrison Ford, Carrie Fisher, Billy Dee Williams, Frank Oz, Alec Guinness

The Empire Strikes Back is a worthy sequel to *Star Wars*, equal in both technical mastery and characterization,

***Robotic stars C3PO (left) and R2D2 return to the screen in the Star Wars** sequel,* **The Empire Strikes Back.**

suffering only from the familiarity with the effects generated in the original and imitated too much by others.

From the first burst of John Williams' powerful score and the receding opening title crawl, we are back in pleasant surroundings and anxious for a good time.

This is exec producer George Lucas' world. Though he has turned the director's chair and his typewriter, there are no recognizable deviations from the path marked by Lucas and producer Gary Kurtz.

They're assisted again by good performances from Mark Hamill, Harrison Ford and Carrie Fisher. And even the ominous Darth Vader (David Prowse [voiced by James Earl Jones]) is fleshed with new – and surprising – motivations.

Among the new characters, Billy Dee Williams gets a good turn as a duplicitous but likeable villain-ally and Frank Oz is fascinating as sort of a guru for the Force.

Vader's admirals now look even more dressed like Japanese admirals of the fleet intercut with Hamill's scrambling fighter pilots who wouldn't look too out of place on any Marine base today.

ENEMY MINE

1985, 108 mins, ◇ Ⓥ   *Dir* Wolfgang Petersen   US

★ **Stars** Dennis Quaid, Louis Gossett Jr, Brion James, Richard Marcus, Carolyn McCormick, Bumper Robinson

Enemy Mine is a friendship story between two disparate personalities carried to extreme lengths. It may be a long way to go to a distant sun system to get to a familiar place, but the $33 million project is largely successful in establishing a satisfying bond.

Story is set up by a kind of videogame battle between the Earth forces and the war-ring Dracs from the distant planet of Dracon. Space pilot Willis Davidge (Dennis Quaid) goes down with a Drac ship and is the only survivor on a desolate planet. His initial response to the half-human, half-reptilian is inbred hatred, distrust and combativeness, all recognizable human triggers.

Hostility soon gives way to a common goal – survival. Davidge and the Drac (Louis Gossett Jr) peel away their outer layers and reveal two similar beings. It's an anthropomorphic view of life but touching nonetheless.

ERASERHEAD

1977, 100 mins, Ⓥ   *Dir* David Lynch   US

★ **Stars** Jack Nance, Charlotte Stewart, Jeanne Bates, Allen Josephs, Judith Anna Roberts, Laurel Near

Eraserhead is a sickening bad-taste exercise made by David Lynch under the auspices of the American Film Institute.

Set, apparently, in some undefined apocalyptic future era, *Eraserhead* consists mostly of a man sitting in a room trying to figure out what to do with his horribly mutated child. Lynch keeps throwing in graphic close-ups of the piteous creature, and pulls out all gory stops in the unwatchable climax.

Like a lot of AFI efforts, the pic has good tech values (particularly the inventive sound mixing), but little substance or subtlety, The mind boggles to learn that Lynch labored on this pic for five years.

E

Dennis Quaid's Earthman comforts Louis Gossett's alien in the planetary parable **Enemy Mine.**

ESCAPE FROM NEW YORK

1981, 99 mins, ◇ *Dir* John Carpenter   US

★ **Stars** Kurt Russell, Lee Van Cleef, Ernest Borgnine, Donald Pleasence, Isaac Hayes, Harry Dean Stanton

Although execution doesn't quite live up to the fabulous premise, *Escape from New York* is a solidly satisfying actioner. Impressively produced for $7 million, it reps director John Carpenter's biggest budget to date.

In the 1997 New York City neatly turned out (mostly in St Louis) by production designer Joe Alves, Manhattan is a walled, maximum security prison inhabited by millions of felons and loonies. The president of the US has the misfortune of crash landing on the island and being taken hostage by the crazies, who demand their release in exchange for the leader.

Into this cesspool is sent tough criminal Kurt Russell, who is charged with extricating the prexy within 24 hours.

Pic only falls a little short in not taking certain scenes to their dramatic limits. For instance, Russell is finally captured by Isaac Hayes and his cronies and thrown, like a doomed gladiator, into an arena with a hulking behemoth. Instead of milking the confrontation for all it's worth, Carpenter keeps cutting away to parallel events elsewhere.

Model and matte work, executed at New World's special effects studio in Venice, is obvious but imaginatively fun enough to get by.

The horribly mutated child from David Lynch's cult creepy **Eraserhead.**

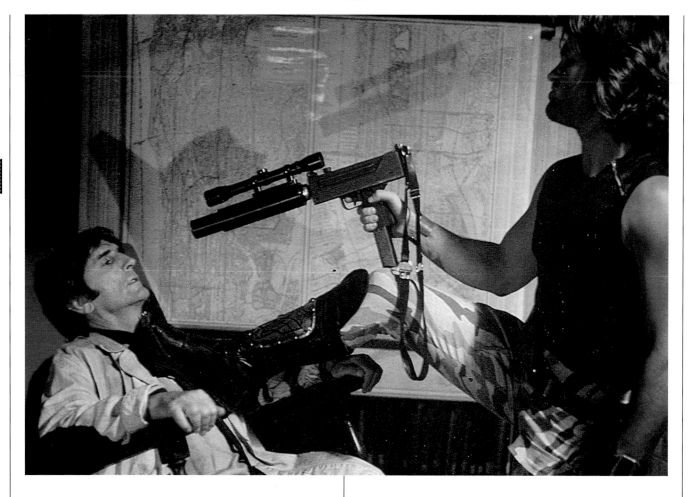

ESCAPE FROM THE PLANET OF THE APES

1971, 97 mins, ◇ Ⓥ *Dir* Don Taylor   US

★ *Stars* Roddy McDowall, Kim Hunter, Bradford Dillman, Natalie Trundy, Eric Braeden, William Windom

Escape from the Planet of the Apes is an excellent film, almost as good as the original *Planet of the Apes*. Arthur Jacobs' production is marked by an outstanding script, using some of the original Pierre Boulle novel characters; excellent direction by Don Taylor; and superior performances from a cast headed by encoring Roddy McDowall and Kim Hunter.

In the previous film one will recall that the world seemed to be ending in nuclear holocaust. Something that trivial never stopped a good writer, so this film opens with Hunter, McDowall and Sal Mineo arriving on earth in a space vehicle.

After about half way through the film's literate, suspenseful, delightful and thought-provoking 97 minutes, the story emphasis segues from broad comedic antics to a rather horrifying dilemma.

Eric Braeden, scientific advisor to US President William Windom, suggests that, if indeed in our future apes would subdue humans, why not remove that distant threat by aborting the life of the child of McDowall and Hunter?

Kurt Russell (right) and Harry Dean Stanton in John Carpenter's apocalyptic actioner Escape from New York.

ESCAPE TO WITCH MOUNTAIN

1975, 97 mins, ◇ *Dir* John Hough   US

★ *Stars* Eddie Albert, Ray Milland, Donald Pleasence, Kim Richards, Ike Eisenmann, Walter Barnes

The two leading protagonists are a young orphaned brother and sister who are psychic.

Based on a book by Alexander Key and directed with a light and sure hand by John Hough, picks up the youngsters as they arrive at a children's home after the loss of their foster parents.

Their unusual powers, displayed early when they warn a man not to enter a car moments before it is demolished by a runaway truck, leads to an eccentric tycoon who craves a gifted clairvoyant who can make him omnipotent, arranging for their transfer to his palatial home where they are held prisoner.

Using their magical talents for an escape, they take up with a cranky oldtimer travelling in a motor home. Much of the action focuses on their efforts to elude the millionaire and his men who want the children returned.

Eddie Albert inserts just the proper type of crankiness as the camper-owner who gets entangled with them, and Ray Milland properly hams the multimillionaire. Donald Pleasence scores, too, as Milland's aide.

ETERNITY

1990, 125 mins, ◇ ⓥ *Dir* Steven Paul   US

★ *Stars* Jon Voight, Armand Assante, Eileen Davidson, Wilford Brimley, Kaye Ballard, Joey Villa

Written in collaboration with director Steven Paul and his mother Dorothy Koster Paul, Jon Voight's vision of mankind's dilemma revolves around mystical notions of reincarnation. Opening reel is a medieval prolog in which Voight wars with his brother Armand Assante over a kingdom, resulting in the death of his beloved Eileen Davidson.

Voight wakes up and, in true *Wizard of Oz* style, recognizes all the people in his life as reincarnations of relatives and other folks from the dream. Assante is now a megalomaniacal, right-wing industrialist out to control the media, the US presidency, and to push a vast weapons project he believes will deter war.

Voight is a self-professed do-gooder, who opposes Assante's militaristic approach. Assante attempts to buy out

The wonder of childhood: close encounter between Henry Thomas (right) and **E.T. The Extra-Terrestrial.**

Voight's show to silence him and then co-opts his girlfriend (Davidson again) by making her a TV star on his network.

Voight invests equal measures of naturalism and quirks in his messianic role which goes over the top occasionally. Davidson stands out in the supporting cast, possessing an unusual beauty reminiscent of Polish star Joanna Pacula.

E.T. THE EXTRA-TERRESTRIAL

1982, 115 mins, ◇ ⓥ *Dir* Steven Spielberg   US

★ *Stars* Dee Wallace, Henry Thomas, Peter Coyote, Robert MacNaughton, Drew Barrymore, K.C. Martel

Academy Award 1982: Best Picture (Nomination)

E.T. may be the best Disney film Disney never made. Captivating, endearingly optimistic and magical at times, Steven Spielberg's fantasy is about a stranded alien from outer space protected by three kids until it can arrange for passage home.

E.T. is highly fortunate to be found by young Henry Thomas who, after some understandable initial fright, takes the 'goblin' in, first as a sort of pet and then as a friend he must guard against the more preying elements of human society. Over time, Thomas teaches E.T. how to talk and includes his older brother (Robert MacNaughton) and younger sister (Drew Barrymore) in on the secret.

Ultimately, of course, the official representatives of society locate E.T., which seems to occasion a rapid decline in its health until it appears to die.

River Phoenix, Jason Presson and Ethan Hawke go on a space mission and meet bug-eyed aliens in **The Explorers.**

As superlatively created by Carlo Rambaldi, the creature manages to project both a wondrous childlike quality and a sense of superior powers. It even gets to play a drunk scene, perhaps a first for screen aliens.

All performers fulfill the requirements, and Thomas is perfect in the lead, playing the childhood equivalent of Spielberg's everyman heroes of his previous pics.

EXPLORERS

1985, 109 mins, ◇ Ⓥ *Dir* Joe Dante   US

★ **Stars** Ethan Hawke, River Phoenix, Jason Presson, Amanda Peterson, Dick Miller, Robert Picardo

Two young boys, a dreamer (Ethan Hawke) and a nerdy science genius type (River Phoenix), manage, through combining their talents and happening upon an unusual discovery, to fashion a homemade spacecraft.

In league with a lower-class misfit (Jason Presson) who falls in with them, the lads inventively use a leftover Tilt-A-Whirl as their basic chassis and elaborate upon their design with spare parts of all kinds.

Along with their extracurricular Advanced Shop work, opening hour is occupied with passable but far from original stuff devoted to bullies vs nerds, puppy love and schoolroom antics.

Throughout, director Joe Dante and writer Eric Luke load the proceedings with references to sci-fiers of an earlier day, such as *War of the Worlds*, *This Island Earth*, *Journey to the Center of the Earth* and many others, but this is nothing compared to what happens when the trio of youngsters finally take off into outer space and make contact with an alien race.

FAHRENHEIT 451

1966, 113 mins, ◇ Ⓥ *Dir* Francois Truffaut   UK

★ **Stars** Oskar Werner, Julie Christie, Cyril Cusack, Anton Diffring, Jeremy Spenser, Bee Duffell

With a serious and even terrifying theme, this excursion into sci-fi has been thoughtfully directed by Truffaut and there is adequate evidence of light touches to bring welcome and needed relief to a sombre and scarifying subject.

In author Ray Bradbury's glimpse into the future, books are considered the opium of the people. Their possession is a crime and the state has a squad of firemen to destroy the illicit literature with flame throwers. Fahrenheit 451, it is explained, is the temperature at which books are reduced to ashes.

The yarn develops just a handful of characters, emphasizing the inevitable conflict between state and literate-minded citizens. One of the principals is Montag (Oskar Werner) an obedient and lawful fireman, who does his book destroying job with efficiency and apparent enthusiasm, while his equally law-abiding wife (Julie Christie) spends her days glued to the mural TV screen.

A young probationary school teacher (also played by Christie) whom Montag meets on the monorail while on the way to the fire station, plants the first seeds of doubt in his mind, and from then on he regularly steals the odd book which he reads secretly.

Werner, in the difficult role of the once diffident and ambitious fireman who finally challenges authority, plays the part in low key style which adds to the integrity of the character, and Christie is standout in her dual roles.

Cyril Cusack plays the fire station captain with horrifying dedication, and Anton Diffring is effectively cast as a heavy who has caught Montag in the book stealing act.

FANTASTIC VOYAGE

1966, 100 mins, ◇ Ⓥ *Dir* Richard Fleischer   US

★ *Stars* Stephen Boyd, Raquel Welch, Edmond O'Brien, Donald Pleasence, Arthur O'Connell, Arthur Kennedy

Fantastic Voyage is indeed just that. The lavish production, boasting some brilliant special effects and superior creative efforts, comes across as an entertaining and enlightening

Cyril Cusack (left) and Anton Diffring, firemen who start fires in the book-burning future of Fahrenheit 451.

excursion through inner space – the body of a man.

The original Otto Klement-Jay Lewis Bixby story, adapted by David Duncan, has been updated and fashioned into an intriguing yarn about five people who undergo a process of miniaturization for injection into the bloodstream of a scientist.

The action cross cuts from lifesize medics to the shrunken quintet who encounter, and are endangered by, the miracles of life in the human body.

The competent cast is headed by Stephen Boyd, the US agent who has brought scientist Jean Del Val to America, only to have a last-ditch attempt on latter's life cause the blood clot which necessitates the weird journey to come. Boyd is assigned to join the expedition under the command of Donald Pleasence, a medical specialist in circulatory systems, thus qualifying him as navigator for William Redfield's submarine.

Richard Fleischer's fine direction maintains a zesty pace. Ernest Laszlo's outstanding lensing brings out every lush facet in the superb production values. Over half of the $6.5 million cost went into the special values.

THE FINAL COUNTDOWN

1980, 103 mins, ◇ Ⓥ *Dir* Don Taylor   US

★ *Stars* Kirk Douglas, Martin Sheen, Katharine Ross, James Farentino, Ron O'Neal, Charles Durning

As a documentary on the USS *Nimitz, The Final Countdown* is wonderful. As entertainment, however, it has the feeling of a telepic that strayed onto the big screen. The magnificent production values provided by setting the film on the world's largest nuclear-powered aircraft carrier can't transcend the predictable cleverness of a plot that will seem overly familiar to viewers raised on *Twilight Zone* reruns.

The liberal sympathies typical of the work of Kirk Douglas are evident in his characterization of the ship's commander as a man whose sense of military honor will not allow him to take the opportunity provided him by a mysterious storm – his ship and crew find themselves transported back in time to 6 December 1941, between Pearl Harbor and the Japanese fleet heading to destroy the American naval base and send the US into World War II.

The philosophical issues raised by the film hardly bear much examination, because the patchwork screenplay by two pairs of writers paints each character in too schematic a fashion. Martin Sheen has much more to work with than Douglas, who seems uncharacteristically subdued.

FIRE AND ICE

1983, 81 mins, ◇ Ⓥ *Dir* Ralph Bakshi   US

Ralph Bakshi's animation feature is interesting for two special reasons: (1) the production represents a clear design on Bakshi's part to capture a wider and younger audience and (2) the animation marks the film debut of America's

leading exponent of heroic fantasy art, Frank Frazetta, who co-produced.

Known for his classic comic book and poster art, Frazetta works some of his famous illustrations into the film, such as his *Death Dealer* painting portraying an axe-wielding figure on horseback. Populating an Armageddon embellished with subhumans and flying dragonhawks are a blond hero, Larn; a sensuous-vulnerable dream girl in distress, Teegra; and an icy sorcerer and his willful mother, Lord Nekron and Juliana. Bakshi shot live actors first, to lay the foundation for the animation, in a process called Rotoscope.

FIRST MEN IN THE MOON

1964, 102 mins, ◇ ⑦   *Dir* Nathan Juran   UK

★ *Stars* Edward Judd, Lionel Jeffries, Martha Hyer, Erick Chitty, Betty McDowall, Miles Malleson

Ray Harryhausen and his special effects men have another high old time in this piece of science-fiction hokum filmed in Dynamation. Picture is based on H.G. Wells' novel and has been neatly updated.

Yarn starts with the arrival on the moon of three United Nations astronauts (Yank, Russian and British) amid world excitement. Pride of the astros receives a jolt when they find a small, faded Union Jack on the moon, together with a yellowed manuscript (a bailiff's receipt) with a scrawl which claims the discovery of the moon on behalf of Queen Victoria – date, 1899.

In a home, an aged man (Edward Judd) is tracked down by UN investigators. He tells them the incredible story of how he, his financee and an eccentric professor actually did land on the moon. He and the girl escaped. The professor remained behind to continue his scientific investigations. The three principals play second fiddle to the special effects and art work, which are impressive in color, construction and animation.

FIVE

1951, 93 mins, *Dir* Arch Oboler   US

★ *Stars* William Phipps, Susan Douglas, James Anderson, Charles Lampkin, Earl Lee

Intriguing in theme, but depressing in its assumption. *Five* ranks high in the class of out-of-the-ordinary pix. It is the story of the last five persons on earth, survivors of an atom blast which turns thriving cities into ghost towns.

Writer-producer-director Arch Oboler has injected vivid imagination into the production, but draws a little too much on his radio technique. Principal criticism lies in its dearth of action. However, interest is sustained in suspenseful situations and convincing dialog.

Oboler has selected his characters with care. William Phipps and Susan Douglas are effective as the love interest, with James Anderson doing a commendable job as the

heavy. Charles Lampkin is competent as the sole Negro in a minute white world, while Earl Lee makes the most of his role as a bank teller who because of his horror-stricken mind, believes he's on 'vacation' from his job.

THE 5,000 FINGERS OF DR. T

1953, 89 min, ⑦   *Dir* Roy Rowland   US

★ *Stars* Peter Lind Hayes, Mary Healy, Hans Conried, Tommy Rettig

The mad humor of Dr Seuss (Ted Geisel) has been captured on film in this odd flight into chimerical fiction. Story and conception were shaped by Dr Seuss for the Stanley Kramer unit at Columbia, and he also contributed to the screenplay and did lyrics for the songs composed by Frederick Hollander. Results are sometimes fascinating, more often fanastic.

Of all the wild and weird happenings, the film's standout is the fantastically imaginative dungeon ballet – a mad creation.

Tommy Rettig is the kid who would rather be out playing with his baseball and dog than learning the scales under the tutelage of Hans Conried, the Dr Terwilliker who becomes the villain of the plot. Opening finds the youngster dreaming he is being pursued by strange creatures with butterfly nets in a land full of odd cylinders and mounds, eerie hues and fog.

This new land is a terrifying one, filled with a strong castle in which Dr T conducts a school of piano for the 500 boys he holds prisoner. In the dugeon, deep below the fortress, is a group of miserable creatures, grown green and moldy with age, who were imprisoned because they dared play instruments other than the piano.

Roy Rowland, an expert in the direction of kids shows his skill in handling Rettig and does fairly well by most of the fantasy, although the material is such that it's hard to keep the interest from lagging at times.

FLASH GORDON

1936, 20 mins, ⑦   *Dir* Frederick Stephani   US

★ *Stars* Larry 'Buster' Crabbe, Jean Rogers, Charles Middleton, Priscilla Lawson, John Lipson, Richard Alexander

Universal's serialization of [Alex Raymond's] *Flash Gordon* cartoon character is an unusually ambitious effort. Feature production standard has been maintained as to cast, direction, writing and background.

Scriptwriters had to depend almost entirely on the cartoon strips for material, yet the dialog rings true for most part. Exploits of Flash Gordon on strange planets, his capture by Emperor Ming, struggle of Ming's daughter and Dale Arden for his love, Dr Zarkov's startling electrical contrivances, and the assistance given by King Thun and his lion men all are moulded together into an intriguing chain of events.

The surreal landscapes of dreams permeate the piano-practice nightmare of **The 5,000 Fingers of Dr. T.**

'Buster' Crabbe is well fitted for the title role, a robust, heroic youth who dares almost any danger. Charles Middleton, best known for his western character portrayals, is a happy choice as the cruel Ming. Jean Rogers and Priscilla Lawson, besides being easy on the eyes, are entirely adequate, as Dale Arden and Ming's daughter respectively.

FLASH GORDON

1980, 110 mins, ◇ Ⓥ *Dir* Mike Hodges   UK

★ *Stars* Sam J. Jones, Melody Anderson, Topol, Max Von Sydow, Ornella Muti, Brian Blessed

The expensive new version of *Flash Gordon* is a lot more gaudy, and just as dumb, as the original series starring 'Buster' Crabbe. Sam J. Jones in the title role has even less thespic range than Crabbe, but the badness of his performance is part of the fun of the film.

This film cost around $20 million, a hefty outlay of money for such frivolity.

The big differences between this film and the old serial are the lavish sets and costumes, and the colorful lensing by Gil Taylor, who also did *Star Wars*.

Jones, a former *Playgirl* nude centerfold whose only previous film role was the husband of Bo Derek in '10', lum-

bers vacantly through the part of Flash Gordon with the naivety, fearlessness, and dopey line readings familiar from the 1930s serials.

Film benefits greatly from the adroit performance of Max Von Sydow as Emperor Ming.

FLASH GORDON'S TRIP TO MARS

1938, 20 mins, Ⓥ *Dir* Ford Beebe, Robert Hill   US

★ *Stars* Larry 'Buster' Crabbe, Jean Rogers, Charles Middleton, Frank Shannon, Beatrice Roberts, Richard Alexander

Smart casting and production is evidenced in the job of celluloiding the character already built up by Alex Raymond's newspaper (King Features) comic strip. It stirs the imagination and is far more novel than serials usually.

Yarn (in 15 chapters) has to do with scientist Dr Zarkov (Frank Shannon) and Flash Gordon (Larry 'Buster' Crabbe) scooting up to the planet Mars to stop the gang up there from gradually destroying this earth with a complicated lamp which sucks the nitrogen out of the atmosphere. For romance, a girl (Jean Rogers) is along; for comedy of a minor sort, a loose-limbed newspaper photog (Richard Kerr).

There are rocket planes and strato-planes and death-ray pistols and a heaping variety of other gadgets that will sit the kids on the edges of their seats.

Productionally, the serial is swell. Scenes on Mars are a Roman holiday for scenic and costume designers, and their good work sets off the footage well.

F

Larry 'Buster' Crabbe as **Flash Gordon** *(third from right),* the space-serial **Star Wars** *of its day.*

FLATLINERS

1990, 111 mins, ◇ Ⓥ *Dir* Joel Schumacher   US

★ **Stars** Kiefer Sutherland, Julia Roberts, Kevin Bacon, William Baldwin, Oliver Platt, Kimberly Scott

Death, the ultimate rush, is the target experience for a group of daring young medical students who break on through to the other side – and live to tell about it. A cautionary tale that ends along fairly traditional horror-sci-fi lines, *Flatliners* is a strikingly original, often brilliantly visualized film from director Joel Schumacher and writer Peter Filardi.

Premise is that daring doctor-in-training Nelson (Kiefer Sutherland) decides to make his mark on medicine by stopping his heart and brain ('flatlining', as the lack of vital signs produces a flat line on the EKG and EEG monitors) and then having himself brought back by the gifted medical students he recruits to help him. Initially angry and reluctant, the others end up totally seduced, vying with each other for the chance to go next by offering to flatline the longest.

Problem is, as Nelson discovers, that the curtain of death, once penetrated, doesn't close behind you, and Nelson finds himself haunted by an aggressive demon from another world. Before he can bring himself to admit that his idea wasn't such a good one, all the others but one have gone over.

Sutherland, as always, registers real presence and pulls off a wildly demanding role, but the remarkably gifted Julia Roberts is the film's true grace note as the low-key, private and intensely focused Rachel.

FLESH GORDON

1974, 78 mins, ◇ Ⓥ   *Dir* Howard Ziehm, Michael Benveniste   US

★ **Stars** Jason Williams, Suzanne Fields, Joseph Hudgins, John Hoyt, William Hunt

Puerile is the word for this softcore spoof of the sci-fi serials of the 1930s which, for their time, had genuine merit as audience hair-raisers. By attempting to combine sexplicity and low-level camp, pic emerges as an expensive-looking mish-mash of obvious double entendres, idiotic characterizations and dull situations. Only compensation is flash of bawdy humor.

Title character (played by Jason Williams) heads a group of earthlings out to defeat evil forces on the planet Porno, bent on flooding the universe with chaos-inducing sex rays. Porno is manned by sinister Emperor Wang (William Hunt). Flesh, his girl (Suzanne Fields) and sidekick (Joseph Hudgins) rocket to Porno and encounter various of the emperor's evil minions and a mildly entertaining series of monsters.

THE FLY

1958, 94 mins, ◇ Ⓥ *Dir* Kurt Neumann   US

★ *Stars* Al Hedison, Patricia Owens, Vincent Price, Herbert Marshall, Kathleen Freeman, Betty Lou Gerson

The Fly is a high-budget, beautifully and expensively mounted exploitation picture [derived from a story by George Langelaan].

Al Hedison plays a scientist who has invented a machine that reduces matter to disintegrated atoms and another machine that reassembles the atoms. He explains to his wife (Patricia Owens) that this will enable humans to travel – disintegrated – anywhere in the world at the speed of light. In experimenting on himself, however, a fly gets into the disintegration chamber with him.

When Hedison arrives in the integration chamber, he discovers some of his atoms have been scrambled with the fly's. Hedison has the head and 'arm' of a fly; the fly has the head and arm of the man – each, of course, in his own scale of size. The problem is to catch the fly and rescramble. But before this can happen, Hedison finds the predatory instincts of the insect taking over so he persuades his wife to put him in a high pressure press and snuff out his life.

One strong factor of the picture is its unusual believability. It is told as a mystery suspense story, so that it has a compelling interest aside from its macabre effects. There is an appealing and poignant romance between Owens and Hedison, which adds to the reality of the story, although the flashback technique purposely robs the picture of any doubt about the outcome.

THE FLY

1986, 100 mins, ◇ Ⓥ *Dir* David Cronenberg   US

★ *Stars* Jeff Goldblum, Geena Davis, John Getz, Joy Booshel, Les Carlson

David Cronenberg's remake of the 1958 horror classic *The Fly* is not for the squeamish. Casting Jeff Goldblum was a good choice as he brings a quirky, common touch to the spacey scientist role. Cronenberg gives him a nice girlfriend (Geena Davis), too.

But there's trouble in paradise. Goldblum's got a set of teleporters that he promises will 'change the world as we know it', and indeed, it changes his.

Even though the machinery is not yet perfected, Goldblum, in a moment of drunken jealousy, throws himself in the works. Unbeknownst to him a fly accompanies him on the journey and he starts to metamorphise.

Chris Walas' design for *The Fly* is never less than visually intriguing. Production design by Carol Spier, particularly for Goldblum's warehouse lab, is original and appropriate to the hothouse drama. Cronenberg contains the action well in a limited space with a small cast.

THE FLY II

1989, 105 mins, ◇ Ⓥ *Dir* Chris Walas   US

★ *Stars* Eric Stoltz, Daphne Zuniga, Lee Richardson, John Getz, Frank Turner

The Fly II is an expectedly gory and gooey but mostly plodding sequel to the 1986 hit that was a remake of the 1958 sci-fier that itself spawned two sequels.

After a shock opening in which the late man-fly's son is born within a horrible insect-like encasement, slickly produced pic [story by Mick Garris] generates some promise as little Martin Brundle is raised in laboratory conditions provided by scientific tycoon Anton Bartok (Lee Richardson).

Afflicted with a dramatically accelerated lifecycle, Martin quickly demonstrates genius, and by the age of five emerges fully grown in the person of Eric Stoltz. Martin becomes determined to perfect his father's teleportation machine, which Bartok controls, and also takes an interest in researcher Beth Logan (Daphne Zuniga).

Martin gradually becomes aware that Bartok's motives are far from benign, and simultaneously begins mutating into a hideous beast while retaining his human sensibility.

By the climax, the film more closely comes to resemble *Aliens* than the previous *Fly*, as the transformed Martin hides behind walls and in the ceiling before pouncing on Bartok's goons, chewing them up and spitting them out.

FORBIDDEN PLANET

1956, 98 mins, ◇ Ⓥ *Dir* Fred McLeod Wilcox   US

★ *Stars* Walter Pidgeon, Anne Francis, Leslie Nielsen, Warren Stevens, Jack Kelly, Earl Holliman

Imaginative gadgets galore, plus plenty of suspense and thrills, make the production a top offering in the space travel category. Best of all the gadgets is Robby, the Robot, and he's well-used for some comedy touches.

The conception of space cruisers, space planet terrain, the monstrous self-operating power plant, and of the terribly frightening spectre that threatens the human principals in the story are weird and wonderful.

With all the technical gadgetry on display and carrying the entertainment load, the players are more or less puppets with no great acting demands made. Leslie Nielsen, space cruiser commander, lands on Altair-4 to search for survivors from a previous flight. He finds Walter Pidgeon, super-scientist, and the latter's daughter (Anne Francis) who, with Robby, are the planet's only inhabitants.

Pidgeon, who has gained knowledge beyond usual human limits, wants the rescuers to be gone. Nielsen takes to Francis and she to him, so he determines to seek out the unseen menace.

Credited for the special effects that add the punch to the show are A. Arnold Gillespie, Warren Newcombe, Irving G. Ries and Joshua Meador.

FRANKENSTEIN UNBOUND

1990, 85 mins, ◇ Ⓥ *Dir* Roger Corman   US

★ *Stars* John Hurt, Raul Julia, Bridget Fonda, Nick Brimble, Catherine Rabett, Catherine Corman

Roger Corman's *Frankenstein Unbound* is a competent but uninspired riff on the venerable legend. For Corman, it's also a return trip to modern British sci-fi, adapting a Brian W. Aldiss novel.

John Hurt toplines as a mad scientist in New Los Angeles of 2031, trying to develop a laser weapon that causes objects to implode. Unfortunately, his experiments are causing time slips, violent dislocations including one that suddenly transports Hurt to Switzerland in 1817.

Hurt chances upon Dr Frankenstein in a local pub and

Leslie Nielsen and Anne Francis in **Forbidden Planet,** *a sci-fi adaptation of Shakespeare's 'The Tempest'.*

he's soon visiting gothic folk Mary Godwin (soon to be Shelley), Lord Byron and Percy Shelley. Out on the rampage is Frankenstein's monster, killing people until his creator fabricates a mate for him.

While warring with Frankenstein and his monster, Hurt ultimately identifies with the two, leading to an interesting and somber climax set in icy wastes as in Shelley's original novel.

Though some of the dialog is clutzy, acting is generally good with top honors to Raul Julia as a thoughtful Frankenstein. More single-minded is Hurt's sketchy role.

Bridget Fonda is attractive in the Mary Godwin role, overshadowed by British actress Catherine Rabett, who brings panache to the role of Frankenstein's fiancee, later resurrected as bride for the monster.

THE FURY

1978, 117 mins, ◇ ⓥ *Dir* Brian De Palma   US

★ *Stars* Kirk Douglas, John Cassavetes, Carrie Snodgress, Charles Durning, Amy Irving, Fiona Lewis

The Fury features Kirk Douglas and John Cassavetes as adversaries in an elaborate game of mind control. Director Brian De Palma is on home ground in moving the plot pieces around effectively.

John Farris adapted his novel for the screen. Most viewers will enjoy the razzle-dazzle of the lengthy pursuit by Douglas of son Andrew Stevens, kidnapped by Cassavetes because of his mystical powers. But apart from a few throwaway references to government agencies and psychic phenomena, there is never, anywhere, a coherent exposition of what all the running and jumping is about.

Strong cast also includes Carrie Snodgress as a staffer in Charles Durning's research institute where Amy Irving (also blessed/cursed with psychic powers) is being readied as a substitute for Stevens. Seems that Stevens is freaking out, despite the attentions and care of Fiona Lewis, and he is targeted for elimination.

FUTURE SCHLOCK

1984, 75 mins, ◇ *Dir* Barry Peak, Chris Kiely   AUSTRALIA

★ *Stars* Maryanne Fahey, Michael Bishop, Tracey Callander, Tiriel Mora, Simon Thorpe, Peter Cox

A chaotic, anarchic punk comedy, made on a micro-budget, but with enough going for it to reach its target audience, *Future Schlock* is a mess, but fun.

Set in Melbourne in the 21st century, the pic posits a post-civil war society in which the middleclass suburbanites defeated the non-conformists and then walled them up in a huge ghetto. Action centers around a ghetto watering hole, Alvin's, where the locals meet to do their own thing. Leading lights are Sarah (Maryanne Fahey) and Bear (Michael Bishop) who do a brezzy nightclub act, often directing hostility against suburbanites who drop by on a slumming trip.

Film is a haphazard affair, with variable performances, uneven writing, and rough sound.

FUTUREWORLD

1976, 107 mins, ◇ ⓥ *Dir* Richard T. Heffron   US

★ *Stars* Peter Fonda, Blythe Danner, Arthur Hill, Yul Brynner, Jim Antonio, John Ryan

Pic is a sequel to *Westworld* in which the rebuilt pleasure dome aims at world conquest by extending the robot technology to duplicating business and political figures.

Peter Fonda and Blythe Danner come across very well in their starring roles as investigative reporters on a junket to help promote the rebuilt and enlarged theme park.

The reporters are hosted by Arthur Hill, repping the theme park owners, and John Ryan, the chief scientist. Fonda and Danner eventually discover the world domination plot with the help of Stuart Margolin, one of the few non-robot technicians still employed.

Yul Brynner makes a cameo reappearance as the robot gunslinger so prominent in *Westworld*, a good bridging element between the two pix.

GAS-S-S-S OR IT BECAME NECESSARY TO DESTROY THE WORLD IN ORDER TO SAVE IT

1970, 79 mins, ◇ *Dir* Roger Corman   US

★ *Stars* Robert Corff, Elaine Giftos, Pat Patterson, George Armitage, Alex Wilson, Alan Braunstein

Ostensibly about the actions of the under-25s of the world, as displayed by a sample group in Texas, when an experimental gas kills off all those over that age, most of the screenplay is devoted to moving a group of six young people along the highways to a New Mexican commune where they've heard 'a brave new world' awaits them.

Obstacles appear in the form of automobile rustlers, headed by a character who calls himself Billy the Kid. After a night of rest, recuperation and rocking at a drive-in theatre, they encounter a gang of football players who try to force them to join the team (whose motto is loot, burn and rape), but they escape.

A brief idyll at the commune is threatened when the bunch of fascistic footballers lay siege, but they're converted just in time.

Robert Corff and Elaine Giftos, despite their top billing, devote most of their screen time smiling at and admiring each other's hair, which is almost of equal length.

THE GOLDEN VOYAGE OF SINBAD

1974, 105 mins, ◇ ⓥ *Dir* Gordon Hessler   UK

★ *Stars* John Phillip Law, Caroline Munro, Tom Baker, Douglas Wilmer, Martin Shaw, Gregoire Aslan

An Arabian Nightish saga told with some briskness and opulence for the childish eye, yet ultimately falling short of implied promise as an adventure spree.

As with producer Charles H. Schneer's *Jason and the Argonauts*, Ray Harryhausen encores as co-producer and special effects collaborator. Among his creations: an animated ship's figurehead, a grotesque centaur, a many-armed religious idol and swordplay adversary, and a couple of small bat-like creatures performing intelligence duty for the black artsy heavy of the piece. Good enough conjuring tricks to impress the kids.

Neither story nor running time are belabored under Gordon Hessler's capable direction. And the play-acting is up to snuff for this kind of throwback, in which John Phillip Law impersonates Sinbad with appealing understatement.

THE GOONIES

1985, 111 mins, ◇ Ⓥ *Dir* Richard Donner   US

★ **Stars** Sean Astin, Josh Brolin, Jeff Cohen, Corey Feldman, Kerri Green, Martha Plimpton

Pic's territory is typical small town Steven Spielberg; this time set in a coastal community in Oregon. Story is told from the kids' point-of-view and takes a rather long time to be set in motion.

Brothers Mikey (Sean Astin) and Brand (Josh Brolin) are being forced to leave their home because land developers are foreclosing on their house to build a new country club. The boys are joined by compulsive eater Chuck (Jeff Cohen) and mumbling Mouth (Corey Feldman) for one final adventure together.

Searching through the attic holding museum pieces under the care of their curator father, the boys uncover a pirate treasure map. Sidetracked only temporarily by the nefarious Fratelli family (Robert Davi, Joe Pantoliano, Anne Ramsey), the boys begin their fairytale treasure hunt.

The pirate One-Eyed Willie, it seems, was no one's fool; he left a deadly obstacle course to the treasure. Linking the kids together is their identification as 'Goonies', residents of the boondocks. Handle apparently imbues them with a mystical bond and idealized state of grace.

GREMLINS

1984, 111 mins, ◇ Ⓥ *Dir* Joe Dante   US

★ **Stars** Zach Galligan, Hoyt Axton, Frances Lee MaCain, Phoebe Cates, Polly Holliday, Scott Brady

In what story there is, amiable Hoyt Axton comes across a mysterious creature in Chinatown and takes it home as a Christmas present for his likable teenage son, Zack Galligan. With the gift, he passes along a warning from the inscrutable Chinese that the creature must never get wet, be allowed into the sunshine or fed after midnight.

For a while, all is extremely precious as the little furry thing goes through an array of facial expressions and heart-warming attitudes.

Without giving away too much, suffice to say the creature spawns a townful of evil, snarling, drooling, maniacal killer-creatures who are bound to cause a lot of woe before their predictable downfall. The humans are little more than dress extras for the mechanics.

GREMLINS 2 THE NEW BATCH

1990, 105 mins, ◇ Ⓥ *Dir* Joe Dante

★ *Stars* Zach Galligan, Phoebe Cates, John Glover, Robert Prosky, Robert Picardo, Christopher Lee

Joe Dante & Co. have concocted an hilarious sequel featuring equal parts creature slapstick for the small fry and satirical barbs for adults. The addition of Christopher Lee to the cast as a mad genetics engineering scientist is a most perfect touch.

Film opens with a wrecking ball demolishing Keye Luke's old curiosity shop in downtown Mahattan to make way for another development project by megalomaniac Daniel Camp, played with relish by John Glover.

The cuddly Mogwai creature Gizmo (wonderfully voiced by Howie Mandel) escapes but is immediately captured by twins Don & Dan Stanton as a research subject for

Lee's science lab Splice of Life Inc. The lab is located in the new Clamp Center office building and, when Gizmo gets loose and exposed to water, the first of hundreds of horrific gremlins are unleashed to wreak mayhem.

Gremlins 2 is sans starpower, but its creatures more than make up for the lack of marquee lure. As realized by Rick Baker, the innumerable creations are quite an eyeful.

GROUNDSTAR CONSPIRACY

1972, 95 mins, ◇ Ⓥ *Dir* Lamont Johnson   CANADA

★ *Stars* George Peppard, Michael Sarrazin, Christine Belford, Cliff Potts, James Olson, Tim O'Connor

George Peppard stars as a government agent trying to break up a spy ring. Spectacular locations around Vancouver, plus some excellent and offbeat music by Paul Hoffert, only partially compensate for a script that is as often routine as it is bewildering. Lamont Johnson's direction is one of his lesser efforts.

Matthew Howard adapted L. P. Davies' [novel] *The Alien* into a diffused whodunit. Michael Sarrazin is, or is not, a traitor who worked in a super-secret lab trying to break a computer code. The lab's destruction launches the story.

Hard by the facility is the summer house owned by Christine Belford who, before disappearing completely from the plot, plays an important role in Peppard's trackdown of Sarrazin. There is a lot of rough action and violence, compounded intrigue, and confusing shifts of focus.

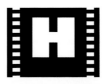

THE HANDMAID'S TALE

1990, 109 mins, ◇ Ⓥ *Dir* Volker Schlondorff   US, W. GERMANY

★ *Stars* Natasha Richardson, Robert Duvall, Faye Dunaway, Aidan Quinn, Elizabeth McGovern, Victoria Tennant

The Handmaid's Tale is a provocative protrait of a future totalitarian theocracy where women have lost all human rights. The adaptation of Margaret Atwood's best seller belongs to that rare category of science-fiction film dealing with dystopias.

Even rarer, *Handmaid's Tale* is sci-fi from a woman's point-of-view. Following a military coup, this future society called Gilead operates under martial law in a perpetual state of warfare (a la *1984*), with Old Testament religion the rule. The so-called sins of late 20th-century society, ranging from

Christmas carols with a difference when the Gremlins call, Joe Dante's cuddly creatures that turned malevolent.

pollution to such activities as birth control and abortion are blamed by the authorities as causing God's plague of infertility, requiring drastic measures to preserve the race.

Natasha Richardson protrays a young mother who's rounded up by the authorities to serve as a breeder, or handmaid, assigned to the barren family of state security chief Robert Duvall and his wife Faye Dunaway. Her travails unfold in Harold Pinter's uncharacteristically staight-forward screenplay rather mechanically.

Although director Volker Schlondorff succeeds in painting the bleakness of this extrapolated future, he fails to create a strong and persistent connection with the heroine's plight.

HAPPILY EVER AFTER

1990, 74 mins, ◇   *Dir* John Howley   US

An unauthorized sequel to the Walt Disney classic *Snow White*, *Happily Ever After* is a well-crafted but uninspired animated fantasy. Lou Scheimer's Filmation banner began work on the pic in 1986 simultaneously with another unauthorized sequel to a Disney masterpiece, *Pinocchio and the Emperor of the Night* (1987).

Action picks up here with the evil queen's brother Lord Maliss (drawn to resemble Basil Rathbone and voiced with gusto by Malcolm McDowell) in a vendetta to avenge sis' death by zonking Snow White and her handsome Prince. Snowy takes refuge in the seven dwarfs' cottage when the

---

Prince is captured. The little fellows are away slaving in the mines, but their femme cousins, the seven dwarfelles, entertain Snowy with their control of natural phenomena.

Voice casting is pic's big plus. Irene Cara warbles a catchy, uptempo song 'Love Is the Reason' to bookend the film. Three other songs spotlight Ed Asner, Phyllis Diller and a very effective vocal from Tracey Ullman simulating a little girl's voice.

HARDWARE

1990, 92 mins, ◇ Ⓥ   *Dir* Richard Stanley   UK, US

★ **Stars** Dylan McDermott, Stacey Travis, John Lynch, William Hootkins, Iggy Pop

A cacophonic, nightmarish variation on the postapocalyptic cautionary genre, *Hardware* has the definite makings of a punk cult film.

After the nuclear holocaust, vast reaches of incinerated North America have been reduced to an infrared desert ravaged by guerrilla warfare and littered with cybernetic scrapheaps. Moses (Dylan McDermott) and Shades (John Lynch) are 'zone tripper' soldiers of fortune who scavenge the corpse-strewn, irradiated wasteland for techno-detritus to black market in the big city.

Moses, wasting away from radiation cancer, wants to return to his woman, Julie (Stacey Travis). She's a fiercely cynical techno-alchemist, fond of smoking packaged dope, who keeps a fortress workshop in a blasted downtown apartment block. Reunited in a frenzied sexual collision of pulse-pounding eroticism, the couple ponder their outer-limits relationship of love in the ruins.

Kyle MacLachlan as taciturn FBI agent Gallagher on the trail of an alien that takes over humans in The Hidden.

All deliver realistic performances. An interesting newcomer is Agneta Eckemyr, cast as a Viking maid.

IT CAME FROM OUTER SPACE

1953, 80 mins, ⬙ *Dir* Jack Arnold   US

★ *Stars* Richard Carlson, Barbara Rush, Charles Drake, Russell Johnson, Kathleen Hughes, Joseph Sawyer

Picture has been smartly fashioned to take advantage of all the tricks of science-fiction and 3-D. Stereo process is not used as just an excuse to pelt an audience with flying objects and, with one exception, when missiles come out of the screen they are tied in logically with the story.

Direction by Jack Arnold whips up an air of suspense and there is considerable atmosphere of reality created, which stands up well enough if the logic of it all is not examined too closely. Some of the threat posed by the landing of visitors from space on earth is lessened when it is established the chance visitors intend no harm.

On the edge of the unknown: a small town faces an alien take-over in It Came From Outer Space.

Otherwise, the Ray Bradbury story proves to be good science-fiction. Yarn opens with Richard Carlson, a scientist, and Barbara Rush, his school-teacher fiancee, observing the landing of a fiery object in the Arizona desert. At first believing it is a meteor, Carlson changes his opinion when he ventures into the crater. Strange things begin to happen in the community. Townspeople disappear and their likenesses are taken over by the space visitors.

Carlson is excellent as the scientist, and Rush makes an attractive partner. Charles Drake is good as the sheriff, and there are some excellent supporting performances.

IT HAPPENED HERE

1964, 99 mins, *Dir* Kevin Brownlow, Andrew Mollo   UK

★ *Stars* Pauline Murray, Sebastian Shaw, Nicolette Bernard, Bart Allison, Stella Kemball, Fiona Leland

It Happened Here tells the story of what might have happened had England been occupied by the Germans. The action takes place in 1943. There's also a story line going through. It centres on the experience of an English nurse who, in order to help, joins the Fascist-controlled Immediate Organization. She soon finds out that her uniform alienates

those around here. She eventually tries to help a wounded partisan. Her action is discovered and she's punished for associating with 'the other side'.

The film shows brutality on both sides. Its message is that Nazism leads to violence everywhere. Film poses the question: can Nazism only be wiped out by Nazi methods?

But despite all controversy, film reveals a tremendous task. Compliments galore should go to the two young men who created it: Kevin Brownlow and Andrew Mollo, the former a professional film editor, the latter assistant director to Tony Richardson who, incidentally, contributed the money to complete the film.

Pic is a non-professional feature which began as an amateur project on 16mm and remained so until financing was secured six years (!) after production had started. The early material was then 'blown-up' and rest of the film shot on standard 35mm. Most of the cast is non-professional. One is hardly aware of this and film cost a mere $20,000.

IT HAPPENED TOMORROW

1944, 84 mins, ⓥ *Dir* Rene Clair   US

★ *Stars* Dick Powell, Linda Darnell, Jack Oakie, Edgar Kennedy

It Happened Tomorrow poses a novel premise on which to spin a comedy-drama – what happens when a cub reporter gets a copy of tomorrow's newspaper. Results provide diverting escapist entertainment, with many sparkling moments and episodes along the line.

Although there are numerous broadly sketched sequences aimed for laugh reaction, picture carries undercurrent of Continental directing technique of Rene Clair. The welding is more than passably successful, but main credit for picture's status can be handed to script by Clair and Dudley Nichols [based on 'originals' by Lord Dunsany, Hugh Wedlock and Howard Snyder, and ideas of Lewis R. Foster]; it picks up every chance for a chuckle or laugh.

Dick Powell, cub on the sheet, is befriended by the rag's veteran librarian who, after death, hands the youth copies of the next day's paper for three successive days.

Interwoven is his meeting and quick romance with Linda Darnell, medium and niece of mindreader Jack Oakie.

IT! THE TERROR FROM BEYOND SPACE

1958, 68 mins, *Dir* Edward L. Cahn   US

★ *Stars* Marshall Thompson, Shawn Smith, Kim Spalding, Ann Doran, Richard Benedict, Ray Corrigan

'It' is a Martian by birth, a Frankenstein by instinct, and a copycat. The monster dies hard, brushing aside grenades, bullets, gas and an atomic pile, before snorting its last snort. It's old stuff, with only a slight twist.

Film starts some dozen years in the future [from 1958] with a disabled US rocketship on Mars. Only one of the 10

space travellers has survived, and a second rocketship has landed to drag him back to Earth where he is to face a court-martial. The government is of the opinion the spaceman murdered his companions so he could hoard the food and stay alive until help arrived. But the accused swears the nine deaths came at the hands of a strange 'It'-type monster.

Most of the film is spent aboard the second rocketship on its way to Earth, and, to spice up the trip, the monster has stowed away. It kills with a swat of its grisly hand, then sucks all available liquids from its victims.

No outstanding performance. Ray 'Crash' Corrigan makes a fetching monster. Technical credits are capable.

JACOB'S LADDER

1990, 113 mins, ◇ ⓥ *Dir* Adrian Lyne   US

★ *Stars* Tim Robbins, Elizabeth Pena, Danny Aiello, Matt Craven, Ving Rhames, Macaulay Culkin

Jacob's Ladder means to be a harrowing thriller about a Vietnam vet (Tim Robbins) bedeviled by strange visions, but the $40 million production is dull, unimaginative and pretentious.

Writer Bruce Joel Rubin (*Ghost*) telegraphs his plot developments and can't resist throwing in supernatural elements that prompt giggles at the most unfortunate moments. Right from the battlefield prolog in Vietnam, where members of Robbins' battalion act strangely and throw fits, it's clear that somebody messed with their brains.

Robbins, whose earnest and touching performance belongs in a better film, spends most of the story struggling to understand the 'demons' pursuing him back home in NY. Director Adrian Lyne adds nothing fresh visually or dramatically to previous film and TV depictions of troubled Viet vets' psyches.

Living in a dim, dingy apartment and working in a dronelike postal service job, Robbins was wrongly told by the army that he was discharged on psychological grounds. His very existence denied by the Veterans Administration, he thinks he's possessed, but eventually pieces together the truth with the help of his battalion buddies.

JASON AND THE ARGONAUTS

1963, 104 mins, ◇ ⓥ *Dir* Don Chaffey   UK

★ *Stars* Todd Armstrong, Nancy Kovack, Gary Raymond, Laurence Naismith, Niall MacGinnis, Douglas Wilmer

Jason and the Argonauts stems from the Greek mythological legend of Jason and his voyage at the helm of the Argo in search of the Golden Fleece. The $3 million film has a workable scenario and has been directed resourcefully and spiritedly by Don Chaffey, under whose leadership a colorful cast performs with zeal.

Among the spectacular mythological landscape and characters brought to life through the ingenuity of illusionist Ray Harryhausen are a remarkably lifelike mobile version of the colossal bronze god, Talos; fluttery personifications of the bat-winged Harpies; a miniature representation of the 'crashing rocks' through which Jason's vessel must cruise; a menacing version of the seven-headed Hydra; a batch of some astonishingly active skeletons who materialize out of the teeth of Hydra; and a passable replica of the Argo itself.

Handsome Todd Armstrong does a commendable job as Jason and Nancy Kovak is beautiful as his Medea.

JOURNEY TO THE CENTER OF THE EARTH

1959, 132 mins, ◇ ⓥ   *Dir* Henry Levin   US

★ *Stars* Pat Boone, James Mason, Arlene Dahl, Diane Baker, Peter Ronson, Thayer David

The Charles Brackett production takes a tongue-in-cheek approach to the Jules Verne story, but there are times when it is difficult to determine whether the filmmakers are

*The Argo encounters one of the denizens of the deep during **Jason and the Argonauts** mythical voyage.*

kidding or playing it straight. The actors neither take themselves nor the picture seriously, which; however; is all on the plus side.

The story concerns an expedition, led by James Mason, who plays a dedicated scientist, to the center of the earth. Among those who descend to the depths with Mason are Pat Boone, one of his students; Arlene Dahl, the widow of a Swedish geologist who steals Mason's information and tries to beat him to the 'underworld'; and Peter Ronson, an Icelandic guide and jack-of-all-trades.

The descent is a treacherous one, filled with all kinds of dangers – underground floods, unusual winds, excessive heat, devious paths. Before reaching their goal, the intrepid explorers confront pre-historic monsters, a forest of mushrooms, a cavern of quartz crystals, and a salt vortex.

Boone is given an opportunity to throw in a couple of songs. Romance is not neglected. Waiting at home in Edinburgh for Boone is Diane Baker, Mason's niece. And it's obvious that Mason and the widow Dahl will end up in a clinch despite their constant bickering during the expedition.

JUBILEE

1978, 103 mins, ◇ ⓥ   *Dir* Derek Jarman   UK

★ *Stars* Jenny Runacre, Jordan, Little Nell, Linda Spurrier, Toyah Wilcox, Ian Charleson

Derek Jarman's *Jubilee* is one of the most original, bold, and exciting features to have come out of Britain in the 1970s.

J

The year is 1578. Queen Elizabeth I is transported by an angel into the future (roughly the present), where she has 'the shadow of the time' revealed to her. Observing a renegade women's collective (a pyromaniac, a punk star, a nympho, a bent historian, etc), Her Majesty watches as the 'ladies' and their friends go about their picaresque misadventures – disrupting a cafe, a punk audition, a murder spree.

Through this process of disemboweling the present through the memory of the past and the anticipation of the future, Jarman unravels the nation's social history in a way that other features haven't even attempted.

At times, amidst the story's violence (there are two vicious killings), black humor, and loose fire hose energy, the film – like the characters – seems to career out of control. Toyah Wilcox, as an over-the-edge firebug, gives the film's finest performance; Jenny Runacre, in a demanding dual role as Elizabeth I and the leader of the collective, is marvelous. And Orlando, as the world-owning impresario Borgia Ginz, steals every scene he's in.

KINGDOM OF THE SPIDERS

1977, 94 mins, ◇ ⊘ *Dir* John Cardos   US

★ *Stars* William Shatner, Tiffany Bolling, Woody Strode, Lieux Dressler, Altovise Davis, David McLean

Though hardly original, *Kingdom of the Spiders* creates its creeps and scares with care, accomplishing exactly what it

Pat Boone surveys the flora and fungi of subterrania in **Journey to the Centre of the Earth.**

sets out to do. The filmmakers have done a job that will satisfy the audience.

On paper, the picture sounds like most of many predecessors: likable scientist William Shatner, helped by beautiful, but capable woman scientist, Tiffany Bolling, find something amiss among the tarantulas of Arizona.

This time it's not nuclear testing, but chemical insecticides that's causing the trouble. Their problem: stop the little beasties before they eat the world.

But Shatner and Bolling work well together on a believable script, adding an amusing mach-feminism clash along the way that's well done.

KING KONG

1933, 100 mins, *Dir* Ernest B. Schoedsack, Merian C. Cooper
US

★ *Stars* Fay Wray, Robert Armstrong, Bruce Cabot, Frank Reicher, Sam Hardy, Noble Johnson

Highly imaginative and super-goofy yarn is mostly about a 50-foot ape who goes for a five-foot blonde. According to the billing the story is 'from an idea conceived' by Merian C. Cooper and Edgar Wallace. For their 'idea' they will have to take a bend in the direction of the late Conan Doyle and his *Lost World*, which is the only picture to which *Kong* can be compared.

Kong is the better picture. It takes a couple of reels for *Kong* to be believed, and until then it doesn't grip. But after the audience becomes used to the machine-like movements and other mechanical flaws in the gigantic animals on view, and become accustomed to the phoney atmosphere, they may commence to feel the power.

Neither the story nor the cast gains more than secondary importance, and not even close. Technical aspects are always on top. The technicians' two big moments arrive in the island jungle, where Kong and other prehistoric creatures reign, and in New York where Kong goes on a bender.

Fay Wray is the blonde who's chased by Kong, grabbed twice, but finally saved. It's a film-long screaming session for her, too much for any actress and any audience. The light hair is a change for Wray. Robert Armstrong, as the explorer, and Bruce Cabot, as the blonde's other boy friend who doesn't make her scream, are the remaining principal characters and snowed under by the technical end.

A gripping and fitting musical score and some impressive sound effects rate with the scenery and mechanism in providing *Kong* with its technical excellence.

KING KONG

1976, 134 mins, ◇ Ⓥ *Dir* John Guillermin   US

★ *Stars* Jeff Bridges, Charles Grodin, Jessica Lange, John Rudolph, Rene Auberjonois, Julius Harris

Faithful in a substantial degree not only to the letter but also the spirit of the 1933 classic for RKO, this $22 million-plus version neatly balances a superb special effects with solid dramatic credibility.

In the original, documentary producer-promoter Robert Armstrong took aspiring actress Fay Wray on an expedition to a lost Pacific Island. A gigantic humanoid gorilla, was found then brought back to civilization where he wasted part of NY searching for Wray.

In Lorenzo Semple's literate modernization, Charles Grodin is the promoter, this time a scheming oil company explorer. Rick Baker is acknowledged for his 'special contributions' to the Kong character: this means that Baker did virtually all of the perfectly-matched and expertly-sized closeups, in which the beast's range of emotions emerges with telling effect.

KING KONG LIVES

1986, 105 mins, ◇ Ⓥ *Dir* John Guillermin   US

★ *Stars* Peter Elliot, George Yiasami, Brian Kerwin, Linda Hamilton, John Ashton

Film leads off with the previous [1976] pic's closing footage. Advancing to the present, the giant ape is stunningly revealed to be breathing via life-support systems. with Linda Hamilton heading a surgical team preparing to give him an artificial heart.

Brian Kerwin arrives from Borneo where he has found a female Kong. He delivers her to the Hamilton group so her blood can be used for the heart transplant operation.

In portraying an Indiana Jones-type figure Kerwin strains for plausibility and film swiftly begins to lose some early credibility. His tough jungle ways are unconvincingly transformed into sensitive concern for both animals.

Meantime the proximity of the two Kongs prompts these primates to discover what comes naturally. This would prove to be the moment when director John Guillermin loses all control of the pic. Mindless chase then proceeds pell mell for the rest of the film, with the army in hot pursuit.

KNIGHTRIDERS

1981, 145 mins, ◇ *Dir* George A. Romero   US

★ *Stars* Ed Harris, Gary Lahti, Tom Savini, Brother Blue, Cynthia Adler

A potentially exciting concept – that of modern-day knights jousting on motorcycles – is all that's good with *Knightriders*. Otherwise, George A. Romero's homage to the Arthurian ideal falls flat in all departments.

Premise is that of an itinerant troupe devoted to ancient principles which pays its way staging Renaissance fairs featuring bloodless jousts. Opening reel or so features one such event in agreeable fashion, even as it plants seeds of dissent within the ranks.

But all Romero can come up with in the way of drama over the next two-plus hours is the spectacle of invidious, greedy big city promoters and agents preying upon the group, with the pure, idealistic King Arthur figure going off to sulk when several of his men are seduced by the notion of becoming media stars.

Both the film's look, with its medieval costumes and bucolic settings, and the long stretches of high-minded talk, most about how pressures to be co-opted into society must be resisted, lend proceedings the air of a hippie reverie.

Another liability is the sullen unsympathetic 'King' of Ed Harris, who is never allowed to project the magnetism or romance expected of such a dreamer.

KRULL

1983, 117 mins, ◇ Ⓥ *Dir* Peter Yates   US

★ *Stars* Ken Marshall, Lysette Anthony, Freddie Jones, Francesca Annis, Alun Armstrong, David Battley

Although inoffensively designed only to please the senses and appeal to one's whimsical sense of adventure, *Krull* nevertheless comes off as a blatantly derivative hodgepodge of *Excalibur* meets *Star Wars*. Lavishly mounted at a reported cost of $27 million, the collection of action set pieces never jells into an absorbing narrative.

Plot is as old as the art of story-telling itself. Young Prince Colwyn (Ken Marshall) falls heir to a besieged kingdom, but must survive a series of tests on the way to rescuing his beautiful bride from the Beast, whose army of slayers imperils his journey every step of the way.

Crucial to Colwyn's quest is his recovery of the glaive, a razor-tipped, spinning boomerang which will enable him to combat the evil Beast. This fancy piece of magical jewelry holds about the same importance as the Excalibur sword did for Arthur.

Professionalism of director Peter Yates, the large array of production and technical talents and, particularly, the mainly British actors keep things from becoming genuinely dull or laughable.

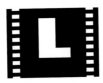

LABYRINTH

1986, 101 mins, ◇ Ⓥ *Dir* Jim Henson   US

★ **Stars** David Bowie, Jennifer Connelly, Toby Froud, Shelley Thompson, Christopher Malcolm, Natalie Finland

An array of bizarre creatures and David Bowie can't save *Labyrinth* from being a crashing bore. Characters created by Jim Henson and his team become annoying rather than endearing.

What is even more disappointing is the failure of the film on a story level. Young Sarah (Jennifer Connelly) embarks on an adventure to recover her baby stepbrother from the clutches of the Goblin King (David Bowie) who has

Ken Marshall brandishes the glaive, a weapon with Excalibur-like qualities, in the fantasy-adventure **Krull.**

taken the child for some unknown reason to his kingdom. Story soon loses its way and never comes close to archetypal myths and fears of great fairytales. Instead it's an unconvincing coming of age saga.

As the Goblin King, Bowie seems a fish out of water – too serious to be campy, too dumb to be serious.

LADYHAWKE

1985, 124 mins, ◇ Ⓥ *Dir* Richard Donner   US

★ **Stars** Matthew Broderick, Rutger Hauer, Michelle Pfeiffer, Leo McKern, John Wood, Ken Hutchison

LadyHawke is a very likable, very well-made fairytale that insists on a wish for its lovers to live happily ever after.

Handsome Rutger Hauer is well-cast as the dark and moody knight who travels with a hawk by day. Lovely Michelle Pfeiffer is perfect as the enchanting beauty who appears by night, always in the vicinity of a vicious but protective wolf.

As readers of one or more variations of this legend will instantly recognize, Pfeiffer is the hawk and Hauer the wolf, each changing form as the sun rises and sets, former lovers cursed to never humanly share the clock together.

The spell was cast by an evil bishop (John Wood) when Pfeiffer spurned him for Hauer, who is now bent on revenge, with the help of young Matthew Broderick, the only one to ever escape Wood's deadly dungeon.

Though simple, the saga moves amidst beautiful surroundings (filmed in Italy), and is worthwhile for its extremely authentic look alone.

THE LAND BEFORE TIME

1988, 66 mins, ◇ ▼ *Dir* Don Bluth   US

Sure, kids like dinosaurs, but beyond that, premise doesn't find far to go. Story is about Littlefoot (Gabriel Damon), an innocent dinosaur tyke who gets separated from his family and after a perilous journey finds them again in a new land.

In this case it's a journey from a dried-up part of the land to another, known as the Great Valley, where the herds frolic in abundant greenery.

After Littlefoot's mother dies, he has to make the journey alone, dodging hazards like earthquakes, volcanoes and a predatory carnivore named Sharptooth. Along the way, he pulls together a band of other little dinosaurs of different species who've been brought up not to associate with each

---

Jennifer Connelly with her allies from the Muppet world of myth-making in Jim Henson's **Labyrinth.**

other. Idea develops that surviving in a changing environment depends on achieving unity among the species. For the most part, pic is about as engaging as what's found on Saturday morning TV.

THE LAND THAT TIME FORGOT

1975, 91 mins, ◇ *Dir* Kevin Connor   UK

★ *Stars* Doug McClure, John McEnery, Susan Penhaligon, Keith Barron, Anthony Ainley, Godfrey James

---

Adapted from Edgar Rice Burroughs' *The Land That Time Forgot* the 'land' in question is an unchartered island, icy on the outside and smoldering within, that's populated with all sorts of big critters.

This island of Caprona is reached by a German submarine which torpedoes an English ship. The survivors, led by Doug McClure, come aboard and capture the sub. But McEnery gets it back. Then McClure takes over again. By this time, it's no wonder the sub is lost in the Antarctic. Luckily, they spot Caprona, easing the sub through an underground tunnel where it's attacked by a Mososaurus.

Somebody identifies the problem here immediately. 'This can't be. These creatures have been extinct for millions of years.'

*The climactic sequence of **The Last Starfighter**, the story of a video game player who becomes a fighter pilot.*

THE LAST STARFIGHTER

1984, 100 mins, ◇ Ⓥ *Dir* Nick Castle   US

★ **Stars** Lance Guest, Robert Preston, Dan O'Herlihy, Catherine Mary Stewart, Barbara Bosson, Norman Snow

With *The Last Starfighter*, director Nick Castle and writer Jonathan Betuel have done something so simple it's almost awe-inspiring: they've taken a very human story and accented it with sci-fi special effects, rather than the other way around.

Lance Guest is a teenager with a talent for a lone video game that was somehow dropped off at his mother's run-down, remote trailer park when it should have been delivered to Las Vegas. And when he breaks the record for destroying alien invaders, Guest not only excites the whole trailer park, he attracts a visit from Robert Preston. Preston is perfect as a headhunter for the Star League of Planets, in dire need of fighter pilots to defend the galaxy from evil invaders.

There is never a moment that all of this doesn't seem quite possible, accompanied by plenty of building questions about what's going to happen next.

LEGEND

1985, 94 mins, ◇ Ⓥ *Dir* Ridley Scott   US

★ **Stars** Tom Cruise, Mia Sara, Tim Curry, David Bennent, Alice Playten, Billy Barty

Legend is a fairytale produced on a grand scale, set in some timeless world and peopled with fairies, elves and goblins, plus a spectacularly satisfying Satan. At the same time, the basic premise is alarmingly thin, a compendium of any number of ancient fairytales.

The plot concerns a heroic young peasant, Jack, who takes his sweetheart, Princess Lili, to see the most powerful creatures on earth, the last surviving unicorns. Unknown to the young lovers, Darkness (i.e. The Devil) is using the inno-cence of Lili as a bait to trap and emasculate the wonderful unicorns.

Kids of all ages should be entranced by the magnifi-cent make-up effects of Rob Bottin and his crew, from the smallest elves to the giant Darkness. The latter is unquestion-ably the most impressive depiction of Satan ever brought to the screen. Tim Curry plays him majestically with huge horns, cloved feet, red leathery flesh and yellow eyes, plus a resonantly booming voice. Also registering strongly is David Bennent as a knowing pixie with large, pointed ears.

Ironically, for a film that celebrates nature, *Legend* was almost entirely lensed on the large Bond set at Pinewood (production was interrupted at one stage by a fire which de-stroyed the set).

LEVIATHAN

1989, 98 mins, ◇ ⊘ *Dir* George Pan Cosmates   US

★ *Stars* Peter Weller, Richard Crenna, Amanda Pays, Daniel Stern, Ernie Hudson

Breed an *Alien* with a *Thing*, marinate in salt water and you get *Leviathan*. It's a soggy recycling [story by David Peoples] of gruesome monster attacks unleashed upon a crew of macho men and women confined within a far-flung scientific outpost.

A stock team of six ethnically mixed men and two alluring women is working out of a mining camp 16,000 feet down on the Atlantic floor, and only has a short time to go until heading back to the surface.

In the meantime, one of the crew, the randy Daniel Stern takes ill after investigating the sunken remains of a Russian ship named Leviathan, dies. and begins transforming into a grotesque eel-like creature.

The same fate awaits Lisa Eilbacher, and medic Richard Crenna quickly deduces that some genetic transferral

is going on. Remainder of the action sees crew members doing fierce battle with the ever-growing creature and being horrifically eliminated one by one.

Shot on elaborate sets in Rome, pic boasts impressive production design by Ron Cobb.

LIFEFORCE

1985, 101 mins, ◇ ⊘ *Dir* Tobe Hooper   US

★ *Stars* Steve Railsback, Peter Firth, Frank Finlay, Mathilda May, Patrick Stewart, Michael Gothard

For about the first 10 minutes, this $22.5 million pic indicates it could be a scary sci-fier as Yank and British space travelers discover seemingly human remains in the vicinity of Halley's Comet and attempt to bring home three perfectly preserved specimens.

The astronauts don't make it back but the humanoids do, and one of them, Space Girl (Mathilda May), is possessed of such a spectacularly statuesque physique that she could probably have conquered all of mankind even without her special talents, which include a form of electroshock vampirism and the ability to inhabit other bodies.

Pic [from the novel *The Space Vampires* by Colin Wilson] descends into subpar Agatha Christie territory, as fa-

Jenny Agutter in Logan's Run *helping Michael York and Richard Jordan escape 'renewal'.*

natical inspector Peter Firth and surviving astronaut Steve Railsback scour the countryside for the deadly Space Girl and make a pit stop at an insane asylum to provide for further hysteria.

Even though she turns millions of Londoners into fruitcakes and threatens the entire world, Railsback just can't get the naked Space Girl out of his mind.

In the meantime, Firth makes his way through scores of zombies in a burning London in the hopes of nailing Space Girl.

LIQUID SKY

1982, 118 mins, ◇ ⑰ *Dir* Slava Tsukerman   US

★ *Stars* Anne Carlisle, Paula Sheppard, Susan Doukas, Otto Von Wernherr, Bob Brady, Elaine Grove

Liquid Sky is an odd, yet generally pleasing mixture of punk rock, science-fiction, and black humor. Story centers on Anne Carlisle, a new wave fashion model who inhabits a world of high-decibel noise, drug addicts (title is slang expression for heroin) and casual sex. Although Carlisle is part of the scene, she doesn't embrace any of its vices.

Unbeknownst to the crowd, a pie-plate sized flying saucer takes up residence in the neighborhood. The creature proceeds to eliminate Carlisle's lovers as they reach orgasm. Carlisle assumes she's developed some strange curse. At first she uses this power for revenge but later attempts to warn her skeptical friends.

Created by Russian emigrees living in New York City, *Liquid Sky* possesses a sophisticated sense of humor. Its view of a changing society is offered up in fiercely black comic tones. Neither the new guard nor the old escapes the filmmakers' barbed observations.

LOGAN'S RUN

1976, 118 mins, ◇ ⑦ *Dir* Michael Anderson   US

★ *Stars* Michael York, Richard Jordan, Jenny Agutter, Roscoe Lee Browne, Farrah Fawcett, Michael Anderson Jr

Logan's Run is a rewarding futuristic film that appeals both as spectacular-looking escapist adventure as well as intelligent drama.

Heading the cast are Michael York and Richard Jordan, two members of a security guard force which supervises the life of a domed-in hedonistic civilization all comprised of persons under the age of 30; after that, the civilization's tribal rules call for a ceremony called 'renewal', though nobody's quite sure what that entails.

York, intrigued and abetted by Jenny Agutter, decides to flee, with Jordan. Peter Ustinov is featured as a withered old man living alone on the outside, in the ruins of Washington, DC.

The three young principals and Ustinov come off very well in their roles.

LOOKER

1981, 94 mins, ◇ *Dir* Michael Crichton   US

★ *Stars* Albert Finney, James Coburn, Susan Dey, Leigh Taylor-Young

Writer-director Michael Crichton has used interesting material, public manipulation by computer-generated TV commercials, to create *Looker*, a silly and unconvincing contempo sci-fi thriller.

Albert Finney, sporting a neutral American accent, heads the cast as Dr Larry Roberts, a leading Los Angeles plastic surgeon being set up as the fall guy in a string of murders of beautiful models who happen to be his patients. Bypassing the police detective (Dorian Harewood) on the case, Roberts teams with model Cindy (Susan Dey) to track down the real killers, with Cindy infiltrating a suspicious research institute run by Jennifer Long (Leigh Taylor-Young) as part of the conglomerate Reston Industries headed by John Reston (James Coburn).

Long has been developing the perfect TV commercials, using plastic surgery-augmented beautiful women as models and expanding into computer-generated simulation techniques. Reston has used these experiments to go beyond subliminal advertising to create hypnotic messages that can sell products or even political candidates.

With numerous lapses in credibility, Crichton falls back upon motifs better used in his *Westworld* picture: computer simulations (for robots), TV blurb soundstages (for film backlots) and assorted fancy chases.

THE LOST WORLD

1960, 97 mins, ◇ ⑰ *Dir* Irwin Allen   US

★ *Stars* Michael Rennie, Jill St John, David Hedison, Claude Rains, Fernando Lamas, Richard Haydn

Watching *The Lost World* is tantamount to taking a trip through a Coney Island fun house. The picture's chief attraction is its production gusto. Emphasis on physical and pictorial values makes up, to some extent, for its lack of finesse in the literary and thespic departments.

In translating the Arthur Conan Doyle story to the screen for the second time (after a lapse of 36 years since the first, silent version), Irwin Allen and Charles Bennett have constructed a choppy, topheavy, deliberately-paced screenplay. Allen's direction is not only sluggish but has somehow managed to project more personality into his dinosaurs than into his people.

Among the curious individuals who venture into this treacherous hidden area at the headwaters of the Amazon are Claude Rains, overly affected as Professor George Edward Challenger; Michael Rennie, a bit wooden as a titled playboy with a notorious reputation; Jill St John, ill-at-ease as an adventuress who chooses tight pink capri pants as suitable garb for an Amazonian exploration; David Hedison, bland as a newsman-photog; and Fernando Lamas, unconvincing as a Latin guitar-player and helicopter-operator.

With the exception of one or two mighty ineffectual prehistoric spiders and a general absence of genuine shock or tension, the production is something to behold. The dinosaurs are exceptionally lifelike (although they resemble horned toads and alligators more than dinosaurs) and the violent volcanic scenery (like hot, bubbling chilli sauce) and lush vegetation form backdrops that are more interesting and impressive than the action taking place in front of them.

MAD MAX

1979, 90 mins, ◇ ⓥ *Dir* George Miller   AUSTRALIA

★ *Stars* Mel Gibson, Joanne Samuel, Hugh Keays-Byrne, Steve Bisley, Roger Ward, Vince Gil

Mad Max is an all-stops-out, fast-moving exploitation pic in the tradition of New World/American International productions. The plot is extremely simple. A few years from now (opening title), the Australian countryside is terrorized by marauders who create mayhem on the roads. A crack police force opposes the villains.

Mad Max is one of the fastest and most ruthless of these cops of the future. Max quits the force to take a vacation with his wife and baby. But when The Toecutter's gang kills his wife and child, he dons his leather uniform again to hunt them down.

Stunts themselves would be nothing without a filmmaker behind the camera and George Miller, a lawyer and film buff making his first feature, shows he knows what cinema is all about. The film belongs to the director, cameraman and stunt artists: it's not an actor's piece, though the leads are all effective.

MAD MAX 2

1981, 94 mins, ◇ ⓥ *Dir* George Miller   AUSTRALIA

★ *Stars* Mel Gibson, Bruce Spence, Kjell Nilsson, Emil Minty, Virginia Hey, Vernon Wells

Uncomplicated plot has Max (Mel Gibson), a futuristic version of the western gunslinger, reluctantly throwing in his lot with a communal group whose lifesupport system is a rudimentary refinery in the desert (he needs the gas).

Western parallel continues as the compound is under continual attack from a bunch of marauders led by the gravel-voiced, metal-visored villain Humungus (Kjell Nilsson).

Ever-the-loner Max decides to strike out on his own again, and is saved by his friend the Gyro Captain (Bruce

Spence) who swoops down from the clouds, and takes him back to the safety of the compound

The climactic chase has Max at the wheel of a supertanker in a desperate flight to Paradise 2,000 miles away (the promised land is the tourist resort on the Queensland Gold Coast, an unexpected touch of black humour).

It's a dazzling demolition derby, as men and machines collide and disintegrate, featuring very fine stunt work and special effects.

Director Miller keeps the pic moving with cyclonic force, photography by Dean Semler is first class, editing is supertight, and Brian May's music is stirring.

MAD MAX BEYOND THUNDERDOME

1985, 106 mins, ◇ ⓥ *Dir* George Miller, George Ogilvie
                                              AUSTRALIA

★ *Stars* Mel Gibson, Tina Turner, Angelo Rossitto, Helen Buday, Rod Zuanic, Frank Thring

The third in the series opens strong with Mel Gibson being dislodged from his camel train by low-flying Bruce Spence in an airborne jalopy (providing as much fun here as he did as the gyro Captain in the earlier *Max* films, this time accompanied by Adam Cockburn as his daredevil son).

To retrieve his possessions, Gibson has to confront Tina Turner, the improbably named Aunty, mistress of Bartertown, a bizarre bazaar where anything – up to and including human lives – is traded as the only form of commerce in the post-apocalyptic world.

Turner throws him a challenge: engage in a fight to the death with a giant known as The Blaster (Paul Larsson) in the Thunderdome, a geometric arena which serves as a kind of futuristic Roman Colosseum for the delectation of the local people.

Gibson impressively fleshes out Max, Tina Turner is striking in her role as Aunty (as well as contributing two top-notch songs, which open and close the picture) and the juves are uniformly good.

THE MAN FROM PLANET X

1951, 70 mins, *Dir* Edgar G. Ulmer   US

★ *Stars* Robert Clarke, Margaret Field, Raymond Bond, William Schallert, Roy Engel, Charles Davis

Story is laid on a small Scottish island, cut off from the mainland. Principals are two scientists, the daughter of one, and a newspaperman, there to observe the effect of a strange planet that is swinging close to the earth. No thought of a planetary invasion is in the minds of the observers until the girl accidentally sees a weird creature from out of space. They take the superior being in, try to communicate with him, but one of the scientists, seeing a chance to control the world, upsets the plans.

Edgar Ulmer's direction builds a strong mood and the

suspense is sustained. Cast is mostly excellent in putting over thriller aims.

Robert Clarke is the reporter and does a good job. Margaret Field is acceptable as the girl, and Raymond Bond does well by his scientist character.

THE MAN WHO FELL TO EARTH

1976, 140 mins, ◇ Ⓥ   *Dir* Nicolas Roeg   UK

★ **Stars** David Bowie, Candy Clark, Rip Torn, Buck Henry, Bernie Casey, Jackson D. Kane

Basic plot has David Bowie descend to Earth from another planet to secure water supply for the folks at home. To help achieve this end, he soon uses his superior intelligence to accumulate vast earthbound wealth and power.

It's a story that must be seen and not told, so rich is it in subplots mirroring the 'pure' spaceman's reaction to a corrupt environment. In fact, pic is perhaps too rich a morsel, too cluttered with themes.

Visually and aurally, it's stunning stuff throughout, and Bowie's choice as the ethereal visitor is inspired.

Candy Clark, as his naive but loving mate, performs well in intimate scenes with Bowie, especially the introductory ones, which are among pic highlights.

MAROONED

1969, 134 mins, ◇ Ⓥ   *Dir* John Sturges   US

★ **Stars** Gregory Peck, Richard Crenna, David Janssen, James Franciscus, Gene Hackman, Lee Grant

What happens when a lunar rocket fails to fire for reentry to earth's gravity? The men on such a capsule become lost in

Anarchy in the outback, with Mel Gibson as the lone law enforcer against all odds in **Mad Max 2.**

space. Such is the situation presented in the gripping drama, *Marooned*, a film, [based on a novel by Martin Cardin] which is part documentary, part science-fiction. The film is superbly crafted, taut and a technological cliff-hanger.

The production's major flaw is a hokey old fashioned Hollywood Renfrew-to-the-rescue climax that is dramatically, logically and technologically unconvincing.

For the first four-fifths of his mission, director John Sturges fashions spectacular documentary footage of launchings, on location work at Cape Kennedy, special effects, studio set ups and scenes on close-circuit TV into an edge-of-the-seat drama in which personalities and human conflicts are never subordinated to the hardware.

MEMOIRS OF A SURVIVOR

1981, 117 mins, ◇ *Dir* David Gladwell   UK

★ *Stars* Julie Christie, Christopher Guard, Leonie Mellinger, Debbie Hutchins, Pat Keen, Nigel Hawthorne

Memoirs of a Survivor is a tale of life when the workings of

a city have ground to a near-halt for some unspecified reason. The film [from the novel by South African novelist Doris Lessing] depicts Julie Christie as D, an attractive middle-aged woman living alone in the midst of the chaos occurring around her. She dreams of a Victorian time and can go through a wall to witness events.

A little girl, maybe her, is seen in the rich, gilded interiors adroitly given a candlelight feeling by lenser Walter Lassally. The mother is annoyed at not being able to read, work and find herself while the little girl is somewhat neglected by mom and her austere father who at one time contemplates her undraped body while she is asleep.

But reality is grim. A teenage girl is moved in with D and she takes care of her. The girl becomes involved with a young man trying to help vagrant children, living in an abandoned subway station. They have already killed one of his helpers and cannibalized others.

People are leaving the stricken city with some indications of an outside government that gives orders. Strife is not due to any atomic war but just communal life running down.

Christie emerges as a fine character player despite her still potent attractiveness. Director David Gladwell apparently did not have the budget to give a more solid look to the degenerating city.

In a story verging on religious allegory, David Bowie (right) was perfectly cast as **The Man Who Fell To Earth.**

METEOR

1979, 103 mins, ◇ Ⓥ *Dir* Ronald Neame   US

★ **Stars** Sean Connery, Natalie Wood, Karl Malden, Brian Keith, Martin Landau, Trevor Howard

Meteor really combines several disasters in one continuous cinematic bummer. Along with the threat of a five-mile-wide asteroid speeding towards earth, with smaller splinters preceding it, there's an avalanche, an earthquake, a tidal wave and a giant mud bath. All in all, special effects wizards Glen Robinson and Robert Staples, along with stunt coordinator Roger Greed, got a good workout.

Inevitably, topliners Sean Connery as an American scientist, Brian Keith as his Soviet counterpart, and Natalie Wood as the translator in between them, take a back seat to the effects.

Avalanche sequence is one of the best in memory, aided by the fact that producers were allowed to blow up a mountain in the Swiss Alps.

MOON ZERO TWO

1969, 100 mins, ◇ *Dir* Roy Ward Baker   UK

★ **Stars** James Olson, Catherine Schell, Warren Mitchell, Adrienne Corri, Bernard Bresslaw, Dudley Foster

Moon Zero Two [from an original story by Gavin Lyall, Frank Hardman and Martin Davison] never makes up its mind whether it is a spoof or a straightforward space-adventure yarn. Overall it's a fairly dull experience, despite some capable artwork and special effects.

The pic, as a 'space western; proposes to show what the moon's probably going to be like in 2021 A.D. and the prediction's not promising.

Space travel has progressed by 2021, and the moon's virtually oldhat. First man to set foot on Mars (James Olson) declines to work as a regular passenger pilot on the Earth-Moon route, preferring to be a freelance explorer, but needs a new spaceship otherwise his girl friend (Adrienne Corri) plans to have him grounded.

Final sequence offers a spot of excitement, but the whole film tends to limp. Moon City's airport, its Wild West saloon and other amenities are presumably meant to be satire but it doesn't come off.

Olson is a melancholy hero. Mitchell plays with tongue in cheek, Bernard Bresslaw as one of his thugs seems bewildered by the entire proceedings.

MY STEPMOTHER IS AN ALIEN

1988, 108 mins, ◇ Ⓥ *Dir* Richard Benjamin   US

★ **Stars** Dan Aykroyd, Kim Basinger, Jon Lovitz, Alyson Hannigan, Joseph Maher

My Stepmother Is an Alien is a failed attempt to mix many of the film genres associated with the 'alien' idea into a sprightly romp.

Dan Aykroyd, as a rumpled, overweight, widower scientist, foils one of his own experiments using lightning and a high-powered satellite dish which results in a signal reaching beyond our galaxy to a planet in peril.

Soon afterwards, a flying saucer lands on a Southern California beach and two aliens alight. They come in the form of quintessential American beauty Kim Basinger in a slinky red sheath dress with an alien-buddy-mentor (the snake, voice courtesy of Ann Prentiss) hiding in her purse.

Their mission is to get Aykroyd to repeat his experiment, which will save their planet.

It is the lengths to which Basinger is expected to go wending her way into Aykroyd's otherwise nerdy suburban lifestyle that is supposed to levitate this fish-out-of-water story to comedic heights.

Mysterious Island *is ambitious adaptation of the Jules Verne yarn that includes giant sea creatures.*

MYSTERIOUS ISLAND

1962, 100 mins, ◇ Ⓥ *Dir* Cy Endfield   UK

★ *Stars* Michael Craig, Joan Greenwood, Michael Callan, Gary Merrill, Herbert Lom, Percy Herbert

Produced in England under Cy Endfield's vigorous direction, the film illustrates the strange plight that befalls three Union soldiers, a newspaperman and a Rebel who, in 1865, escape the siege of Richmond in the inevitable Jules Verne balloon and return to land on an island in the remote South Seas, where they encounter, in chronological order: (1) a giant crab, (2) a giant bird, (3) two lovely shipwrecked British ladies of average proportions, (4) a giant bee, (5) a band of cut-throat pirates, (6) Captain Nemo's inoperative sub, (7) Captain Nemo. The screenplay, from Verne's novel, winds with a staple of the science-fantasy melodrama –74 an entire volcanic isle sinking into the sea as the heroes and heroines beat a hasty retreat.

Dramatically the film is awkward, burdened with unanswered questions and some awfully ineffectual giant animals, but photographically it is noteworthy for the Super-dynamation process and special visual effects by Ray Harryhausen.

THE NAVIGATOR

1988, 93 mins, ◇ Ⓥ *Dir* Vincent Ward   NEW ZEALAND

★ *Stars* Bruce Lyons, Chris Haywood, Hamish McFarlane, Marshall Napier, Noel Appleby

The Navigator is remarkable because of its absorbing story that links medieval fears and fortunes to our times, while confirming director Vincent Ward as an original talent.

The story begins in Cumbria in 1348, the year of the Black Death. Young Griffin (Hamish McFarlane) is anxious for the return of his beloved, much-older brother Connor (Bruce Lyons) from the outside world. He is haunted by a dream about a journey, a quest to a great cathedral in a celestial city, and a figure about to fall from a steeple.

When his brother returns to the village with tales of impending doom, the two brothers, with four comrades, set out on the journey fired by Griffin's prophetic dream. It takes them to a city of the late 1980s and on a mission against time if their village is to be saved.

The formidable skills of Ward are shown in the way his story works, not only as adventure, but as the love story of two brothers and a parable of faith and religion.

Geoffrey Simpson's photography – stark black and white for the Cumbrian sequences, color for the enactment of Griffin's dream and visions – is of the highest order, with score by Iranian composer Davood Tabrizi (domiciled in Sydney) empathetic with the whole.

THE NEPTUNE FACTOR

1973, 98 mins, ◇ Ⓥ   *Dir* Daniel Petrie   CANADA

★ *Stars* Ben Gazzara, Yvette Mimieux, Walter Pidgeon, Ernest Borgnine

The Neptune Factor is an under-sea sci-fi potboiler loaded with interesting technology and kindergarten plotting. Production, made in Canada, has a dull script, dreary direction by Daniel Petrie and a cast of familiar names for whom audiences may feel some embarrassment.

Script traces the rescue of some underwater scientists whose sea-bottom lab is hurled into an ocean crevasse by an earthquake. The action lurches from the surface control ship where Walter Pidgeon and Yvette Mimieux are anxious observers, to the underwater rescue vehicle, skippered by Ben Gazzara whose crew includes Ernest Borgnine and Donnelly

Rhodes, fellow scientists of the lost crew who are determined to find them.

Gazzara's role demands he project cool concern most of the time; Borgnine, Pidgeon and the others gove it the old college try.

THE NEVERENDING STORY

1984, 94 mins, ◇ Ⓥ *Dir* Wolfgang Petersen   W.GERMANY

★ *Stars* Noah Hathaway, Barret Oliver, Tami Stronach, Moses Gunn, Patricia Hayes, Sydney Bromley

Wolfgang Petersen's *Neverending Story* is a marvelously realized flight of pure fantasy.

With the support of top German, British and US technicians and artists plus a hefty $27 million budget (highest for any film made outside US or USSR), helmer Petersen has improved on pic's immediate forbear, Jim Henson/Frank Oz 1982 *The Dark Crystal*, by avoiding too much unrelieved strangeness.

Film opens with a little boy, Bastian (Barret Oliver), borrowing a strange-looking book at a local bookstore and holes up in the school attic to read.

Book, titled *The Neverending Story* depicts a world known as Fantasia, threatened by an advancing force called The Nothing (represented by storms) which is gradually destroying all. To save Fantasia, an ailing empress (Tami

Hamish McFarlane in **The Navigator,** *a story of 'time travel' spanning six centuries.*

Stronach) sends for a young warrior from among the plains people, Atreyu (Noah Hathaway) to go on a quest to find a cure for her illness.

Filming at and backed by Bavaria Studios, *Story* benefits from special effects technicians working overtime to create a new-look world.

THE NEVERENDING STORY II THE NEXT CHAPTER

1990, 89 mins, ◇ ⓥ *Dir* George Miller   GERMANY

★ *Stars* Jonathan Brandis, Kenny Morrison, Clarissa Burt, Alexandra Johnes, Martin Umbach, John Wesley Shiff

Follow-up, produced by Germans based in Munich with location filming in Canada, Argentina, Australia, France and Italy, is a natural, since first film directed by Wolfgang Petersen only covered half of Michael Ende's classic novel.

Part II utilizes a whole new cast (except for Thomas Hill, reprising as Koreander the bookseller) to depict adventures in the imaginary world of Fantasia. Main innovation is that young hero Bastian joins his fantasy counterpart Atreyu in a heroic trek in search of the childlike empress locked in her Ivory Tower in Fantasia, rather than just reading about him.

Another improvement is the inclusion of a delicious villainess, dark beauty Clarissa Burt as Xayide, who suckers Bastian into making numerous wishes, each time losing a bit of his memory in return.

Film is effective in its own right, but as with most sequels, it lacks freshess. American actress Burt is any adoles-

cent boy's fantasy seductress. Rest of the cast is adequate, but a letdown compared with the original's.

1984

1956, 90 mins, *Dir* Michael Anderson   UK

★ *Stars* Michael Redgrave, Edmond O'Brien, Jan Sterling, David Kossoff, Mervyn Johns, Donald Pleasence

A sinister glimpse of the future as envisaged by George Orwell, *1984* is a grim, depressing picture about the world divided into three major powers following an atomic war.

London, the setting for the story, is the capital of Oceania and is run by a ruthless regime, the heads of which are members of the inner party while their supporters are in the outer party. There are ministeries of Love and Thought, anti-sex leagues and record divisions where the speeches of the great are rewritten from time to time to suit the needs of contemporary events.

The story is built around the illegal romance of two members of the outer party, Edmond O'Brien; playing the part of Winston Smith; and Jan Sterling as Julia.

Orwell's picture of the ultimate in totalitarian ruthlessness is faithfully presented. Television 'eyes' keep a day-and-night watch on party members in their homes and TV screens are to be found everywhere, blurting out the latest reports on the endless wars with rival powers.

The Neverending Story II *had newcomer Jonathan Brandis in the role of the adventure-prone boy Bastian.*

Above: 'Big Brother Is Watching You'. The Fifties film version of George Orwell's 1984.

Below: Richard Burton as O'Brien (right) and John Hurt as Smith in the 1984 version of Nineteen Eighty-Four.

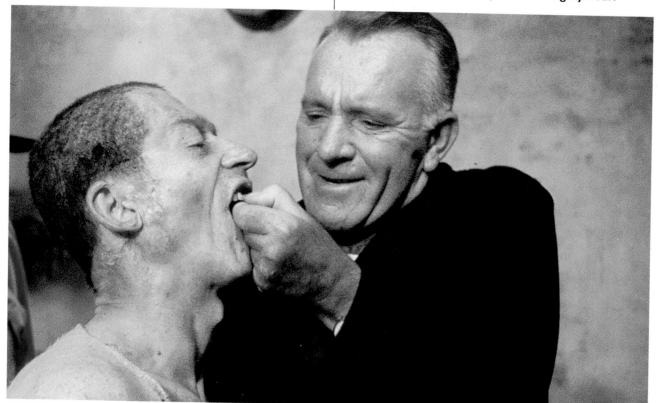

NINETEEN EIGHTY-FOUR

1984, 120 mins, ◇ Ⓥ *Dir* Michael Radford   UK

★ *Stars* John Hurt, Richard Burton, Suzanna Hamilton, Cyril Cusack, Gregor Fisher, James Walker

In this unremitting downer, writer-director Michael Radford introduces no touches of comedy or facile sensationalism to soften a harsh depiction of life under a totalitarian system as imagined by George Orwell in 1948.

Richard Burton is splendid in his role as inner-party official O'Brien. Ironically, his swansong performance as the deceptively gentle spur to Winston Smith's 'thought-crimes', and then as the all-knowing interrogator who takes on the attributes of a father-figure to the helpless man whom he is intent on destroying, is something new in Burton's repertoire.

Also strong is Suzanna Hamilton as Julia who is the other agent of Smith's downfall. John Hurt as Winston Smith holds center stage throughout.

THE OMEGA MAN

1971, 98 mins, ◇ Ⓥ *Dir* Boris Sagal   US

★ *Stars* Charlton Heston, Anthony Zerbe, Rosalind Cash, Paul Koslo, Lincoln Kilpatrick, Eric Laneuville

The Omega Man is an extremely literate science-fiction drama starring Charlton Heston as the only survivor of a worldwide bacteriological war, circa 1975. Thrust of the well-written story [adapted from Richard Matheson's novel] is Heston's running battle with deranged survivors headed by Anthony Zerbe.

The deserted streets of LA through which Heston drives by day while Zerbe's eye-sensitive mutations hide until nightfall, provide low-key but powerful emphasis on what can and does happen when the machinery of civilized society grinds to a halt.

An Oriental missile war has resulted in a worldwide plague. Zerbe, formerly a TV newscaster, has become the leader of the mutations, whose extreme reaction to the science which caused the horrific disaster has led to the wanton destruction of all cultural and scientific objects. Rosalind Cash provides romantic interest for Heston as a member of another band of rural survivors not yet come under Zerbe's control.

Charlton Heston is **The Omega Man,** *the only survivor, apart from mutants, from bacteriological war.*

ONE MILLION B.C.

1940, 80 mins, Ⓥ *Dir* Hal Roach, Hal Roach Jr   US

★ *Stars* Victor Mature, Carole Landis, Lon Chaney Jr, John Hubbard, Mamo Clark, Nigel de Brulier

One Million B.C. looks something like A.D.1910; it's that corny. Except for the strange-sounding grunts and monosyllabic dialog, it is also another silent. Hal Roach, who spent a lifetime making comedies, goes to the other extreme as producer of the prehistoric spectacle, filmed in Nevada. D.W. Griffith was associated with Roach in production of the film at the beginning but withdrew following dissension concerning casting and other angles. His name does not appear in the credits.

There isn't much sense to the action nor much interest in the characters. Majority of the animals fail to impress but the fight between a couple of lizards, magnified into great size, is exciting and well photographed. The ease with which some of the monsters are destroyed by man is a big laugh, notably the way one is subdued with a fishing spear. Knocking off a giant iguana is another audience snicker.

On occasion, also, the actions of the characters, including Victor Mature, bring a guffaw. He plays the part ox-like and the romantic interest, with Carole Landis on the other end, fails to ignite. Chaney Jr carves a fine characterization from the role of a tribal chieftain.

The story, pretty thin, relates to the way common dangers serve to wash up hostilities between the Rock and Shell clans, with a note of culture developed by the heroine (Landis) who astonishes the lads of the stone age when she sees to it that the women are to be served first, and the roast dinosaur (or whatever it is) is cut off in hunks with a rock knife, instead of torn off by the hands.

ONE MILLION YEARS B.C.

1966, 100 mins, ◇ ⦵ *Dir* Don Chaffey   UK

★ *Stars* Raquel Welch, John Richardson, Percy Herbert, Robert Brown, Martine Beswick, Jean Wladon

Biggest novelty gimmick is that, despite four writers on screenplay [Mickell Novak, George Baker and Joseph Frickert from 1940 screenplay *One Million B.C.*, plus producer Michael Carreras], dialog is minimal, consisting almost entirely of grunts. Raquel Welch here gets little opportunity to prove herself an actress but she is certainly there in the looks department.

Also known as **Man and his Mate,** *Victor Mature (as the former) carries off Carole Landis in* **One Million B.C.**

Don Chaffey does a reliable job directorially, but leans heavily on the ingenious special effects in the shape of prehistoric animals and a striking earthquake dreamed up by Ray Harryhausen. Simple idea of the film is of the earth as a barren, hostile place, one million years B.C., inhabited by two tribes, the aggressive Rock People and the more intelligent, gentler Shell People.

John Richardson plays a Rock man who is banished after a fight with his gross father (Robert Brown). Wandering the land, battling off fearful rubber prehistoric monsters, he comes across the Shell People and falls for Welch, one of the Shell handmaidens. The two go off together to face innumerable other hazards.

ONE NIGHT STAND

1984, 94 mins, ◇ ⦵ *Dir* John Duigan   AUSTRALIA

★ *Stars* Tyler Coppin, Cassandra Delaney, Jay Hackett, Saskia Post, Midnight Oil

It's New Year's Eve on a hot summer night in Sydney. Over a transistor radio comes the news nobody thought was possible: nuclear war has broken out in Europe and North America, and bombs have already dropped on US facilities in Australia: everyone is warned to stay where they are.

Thus begins a long, long night.

Pic builds inexorably to a truly shattering climax, yet doesn't rely on special effects or histrionics. Director John Duigan seems to suggest that, in Australia at least, the world will end not with a bang nor exactly a whimper, but with a puzzled question-mark.

It's a daring approach but overall, and despite some rather strident acting early on, it does work.

ON THE BEACH

1959, 134 mins, ◇ ⦵ *Dir* Stanley Kramer   US

★ *Stars* Gregory Peck, Ava Gardner, Fred Astaire, Anthony Perkins, Donna Anderson, John Tate

On the Beach is a solid film of considerable emotional, as well as cerebral, content. But the fact remains that the final impact is as heavy as a leaden shroud. The spectator is left with the sick feeling that he's had a preview of Armageddon, in which all contestants lost.

John Paxton, who did the screenplay from Nevil Shute's novel, avoids the usual cliches. There is no sergeant from Brooklyn, no handy racial spokesmen. Gregory Peck is a US submarine commander. He and his men have been spared the atomic destruction because their vessel was submerged when the bombs went off.

The locale is Australia and the time is 1964. Nobody remembers how or why the conflict started. 'Somebody pushed a button,' says nuclear scientist Fred Astaire. Australia, for ill-explained reasons, is the last safe spot on earth. It is only a matter of time before the radiation hits the

Outland, a space action-thriller with Sean Connery as a Western-style sheriff come to clear up the town.

continent and its people die as the rest of the world has already died.

In addition to Peck and Astaire, the other chief characters include Ava Gardner, a pleasure-bent Australian; and a young Australian naval officer and his wife, Anthony Perkins and Donna Anderson. All the personal stories are well-presented. The trouble is it is almost impossible to care with the implicit question ever-present – do they live?

The cast is almost uniformly excellent. Peck and Gardner make a good romantic team in the last days of the planet. Perkins and Anderson evoke sympathy as the young couple. Fred Astaire, in his first straight dramatic role, attracts considerable attention.

OUTLAND

1981, 109 mins, ◇   *Dir* Peter Hyams   US

★ **Stars** Sean Connery, Peter Boyle, Frances Sternhagen, Kika Markham

Outland is something akin to *High Noon* in outer space, a simple good guys–bad guys yarn set in the future on a volcanic moon of Jupiter.

While there are several mile-wide plot holes and one key under-developed main character, the film emerges as a tight, intriguing old-fashioned drama that gives audiences a hero worth rooting for.

It's clear from the beginning that newly arrived marshal Sean Connery is going to have his hands full. Soon into the action, a miner takes it upon himself to enter the deadly moon atmosphere without his spacesuit and literally fries before the audience's eyes.

Connery soon finds out that the miners are growing crazy due to an amphetamine they are taking that makes them produce more, but eventually destroys their brains. It doesn't take long to figure out that his rival (Peter Boyle), the smug general manager who basically runs the colony's operations, is involved in supplying the drug.

Writer-director Peter Hyams falls just short of providing the exciting payoff to the conflicts he so painstakingly sets up throughout the picture.

PAJAMA PARTY

1964, 82 mins, ◇ ▼   *Dir* Don Weis   US

★ **Stars** Tommy Kirk, Annette Funicello, Elsa Lanchester, Jody McCrea, Buster Keaton, Dorothy Lamour

Exuberance of youth guns the action which twirls around a personable young Martian – Tommy Kirk – arriving on earth to pave the way for an invasion. He lands during a swimming party tossed by an eccentric wealthy widow (Elsa

Lanchester), and immediately falls for Annette Funicello, girl-friend of widow's lug nephew (Jody McCrea).

Funicello displays an engaging presence and registers solidly. Kirk likewise shows class and Lanchester projects a rather zany character nicely, McCrea hams it up the way he should for such a part. Buster Keaton, playing an Indian, and Dorothy Lamour, dress store manager, sock over their roles.

PANIC IN YEAR ZERO

1962, 92 mins, *Dir* Ray Milland   US

★ *Stars* Ray Milland, Jean Hagen, Frankie Avalon, Mary Mitchel, Joan Freeman

The aftermath of a nuclear attack is the subject pursued by this serious, sobering and engrossing film. The screenplay by Joy Simms and John Morton, from a story by the former, advances the theory that, in the event of a sudden wholesale outbreak of nuclear warfare, civilization will swiftly deteriorate into a decentralized society of individual units, each necessarily hostile in relations with all others as part of a desperate struggle for self-preservation.

A family unit of four – father, mother and two teenaged children – is followed here in the wake of a series of initial nuclear blasts destroying Los Angeles and four other major US cities (excluding Washington – a rather astonishing oversight on the part of the unspecified enemy). The family is followed to an isolated cave in the hills where, thanks to the father's negative ingenuity, it remains until it is safe to come out and return home for the enormous task of rebuilding.

Sci-fi-horror pic Parasite, in which a scientist tries to neutralise a strain of parasites he has been developing for the government.

Ray Milland manages capably in the dual task of director and star (he's the resourceful father), but it's safe to observe that he'd probably have done twice as well by halving his assignment, one way or the other.

PARASITE

1982, 85 mins, ◇ Ⓥ *Dir* Charles Band   US

★ *Stars* Robert Glaudini, Demi Moore, Luca Bercovici, James Davidson, Al Fann, Vivian Blaine

Parasite is a low-budget monster film which utilities the 3-D process to amplify its shock effects.

Set in 1992, tale has a skimpy sci-fi peg of scientist Dr Paul Dean (Robert Glaudini) attempting to neutralize a strain of parasite he has developed for the government. Morbid premise is that the large, worm-like parasite is in his abdomen growing while he studies another specimen, racing to somehow avert his own death and save the world from millions of offspring.

Pic's raison d'etre is a set of frightening mechanical and sculpted monster makeup effects created by Stan Winston. Convincing gore and sudden plunges at the camera are greatly enhanced by use of Stereo Vision 3-D filming. Otherwise Parasite is lethargic between its terror scenes, making it a test of patience for all but the fanatical followers of horror cheapies.

PEACEMAKER

1990, 90 mins, ◇ ⑦ *Dir* Kevin S. Tenney   US

★ **Stars** Robert Forster, Lance Edwards, Hilary Shephard, Robert Davi, Bert Remsen

Peacemaker is an unexpected gem of a film. Directed by Kevin Tenney; it is a science-fiction action thriller that really delivers the goods despite an apparent low production budget.

The inventive plot is an exciting tale of two humanoid aliens (Robert Forster and Lance Edwards) who crash-land on Earth. One of them is an inter-galactic serial killer, the other a police officer, or alternatively a peacemaker. A simple set-up, except for one complication: both claim to be the cop.

Both aliens attempt to enlist the aid of assistant medical examiner Hilary Shepard, hoping she can help them find the key to the one functional space rover that survived their crash landing.

Peacemaker is a stunt extravaganza, a nonstop, fast-paced assemblage of chases, shootouts and explosions building to an impressive climax. Pic has a big-budget look throughout.

THE PEOPLE THAT TIME FORGOT

1977, 90 mins, ◇ ⑦ *Dir* Kevin Connor   US

★ **Stars** Patrick Wayne, Doug McClure, Sarah Douglas, Dana Gillespie, Thorley Walters, Shane Rimmer

This is the story of a small party headed by Patrick Wayne seeking a marooned World War I naval hero north of the ice barrier in the Arctic. Film is the second in Edgar Rice Burroughs' *Lost World* trilogy lensed in the Canary Islands and in Britain.

Special effects predominate the action as Wayne and his group leave their ship in a 1918 amphibian through ice-cluttered water and perilously lift over towering ice peaks, are attacked by a giant pterodactyl and forced to crash-land on the dusty island of Caprona.

Again, special effects add to the suspense as the group encounter all manner of hair-raising beasties and erupting fire in braving the dangers of the cavemen in an attempt to find their quarry.

Michael Pare attempts to reverse The Philadelphia Experiment *which projected him into the future.*

THE PHILADELPHIA EXPERIMENT

1984, 102 mins, ◇ Ⓥ *Dir* Stewart Raffill   US

★ *Stars* Michael Pare, Nancy Allen, Eric Christmas, Bobby Di Cicco, Kené Holliday

The Philadelphia Experiment had a lot of script problems in its development that haven't been solved yet, but final result is an adequate sci-fi yarn.

Problems with the pic are common to all stories with a time-warp twist but director Stewart Raffill and writers have kept *Philadelphia* reasonably simple.

In 1943, Michael Pare and Bobby Di Cicco are sailors aboard a destroyer that's the center of a secret radar experiment which goes awry, throwing them into 1984, seemingly cross-circuited into another experiment.

Befriended in the future by Nancy Allen, the pair obviously are a bit bemused at their surroundings before Di Cicco fades again into the past, leaving Pare to develop a romance with Allen and try to find his own way back in time.

Roddy McDowall (left) and Kim Hunter try taming a wild-looking Charlton Heston in Planet of the Apes.

PLANET OF THE APES

1968, 112 mins, ◇ Ⓥ *Dir* Franklin J. Schaffner   US

★ *Stars* Charlton Heston, Roddy McDowall, Kim Hunter, Maurice Evans, James Whitmore, James Daly

Planet of the Apes is an amazing film. A political-sociological allegory, cast in the mold of futuristic science-fiction, it is an intriguing blend of chilling satire, a sometimes ludicrous juxtaposition of human and ape mores, optimism and pessimism.

Pierre Boulle's novel, in which US space explorers find themselves in a world dominated by apes, has been adapted by Michael Wilson and Rod Serling.

The totality of the film works very well, leading to a surprise ending. The suspense, and suspension of belief, engendered is one of the film's biggest assets.

Charlton Heston, leader of an aborted space shot which propels his crew 20 centuries ahead of earth, is a cynical man who eventually has thrust upon him the burden of reasserting man's superiority over all other animals. At fadeout, he is the new Adam.

Key featured players – all in ape makeup – include Roddy McDowall and Kim Hunter, Maurice Evans, James Whitmore and James Daly.

The man-hunting alien returns in Predator 2, but this time to the inner city anarchy of downtown Los Angeles.

PREDATOR

1987, 107 mins, ◇ Ⓥ   *Dir* John McTiernan   US

★ **Stars** Arnold Schwarzenegger, Carl Weathers, Elpidia Carrillo, Bill Duke, Jesse Ventura, Sonny Landham

Predator is a slightly above-average actioner that tries to compensate for tissue-thin-plot with ever-more-grisly death sequences and impressive special effects.

Arnold Schwarzenegger plays Dutch, the leader of a vaguely defined military rescue team that works for allied governments. Called into a US hot spot somewhere in South America, he encounters old buddy Dillon (Carl Weathers), who now works for the CIA.

The unit starts to get decimated in increasingly garish fashion by an otherworldly Predator. Enemy is a nasty, formidable foe with laser powers.

Schwarzenegger, while undeniably appealing, still has a character who's not quite real. While the painted face, cigar, vertical hair and horizontal eyes are all there, none of the humanity gets on the screen, partly because of the sparse dialog.

Weathers can't breathe any life into the cardboard character of Dillon, who goes from being unbelievably cynical to unbelievably heroic in about five minutes.

Director John McTiernan relies a bit too much on special effects 'thermal vision' photography, in looking through the Predator's eyes, while trying to build tension before the blood starts to fly.

PREDATOR 2

1990, 108 mins, ◇ Ⓥ   *Dir* Stephen Hopkins   US

★ **Stars** Danny Glover, Gary Busey, Ruben Blades, Maria Conchita Alonso, Bill Paxton, Kevin Peter Hall

While the film doesn't achieve the same thrills of the final 45 minutes of *Predator* in terms of overall excitement, it outdoes its first safari in start-to-finish hysteria. The real star is the pic's design. Writers don't waste much time on character development.

The setting is Los Angeles, 1997, where outgunned cops face hordes of Jamaican, Colombian and other assorted drug dealers who rule the streets. It's a balmy 109 degrees in the globally warmed basin, where Danny Glover heads a dedicated, ethnically mixed group of cops who are more than a little confused as the drug dealers start turning up dead in droves. The plot thickens when a fed (Gary Busey) comes in to take charge of the investigation.

Centerpiece is, again, a massive alien gifted with the strange weaponry and camouflage abilities like his kinsman that, it's told, had visited the planet 10 years earlier.

The pace of the film is absolutely frenetic. An awe-

inspiring set in the closing sequence recalls the climactic moment in *Aliens*.

THE PRINCESS BRIDE

1987, 98 mins, ◇ Ⓥ   *Dir* Rob Reiner   US

★ **Stars** Cary Elwes, Mandy Patinkin, Chris Sarandon, Christopher Guest, Wallace Shawn

Based on William Goldman's novel, this is a post-modern fairytale that challenges and affirms the conventions of a genre that may not be flexible enough to support such horseplay. It also doesn't help that Cary Elwes and Robin Wright as the loving couple are nearly comatose and inspire little passion from each other, or the audience.

Bound together by their love at tender age, young Westley (Elwes) then stableboy, falls in love with his beautiful mistress (Wright), but they're separated when he goes off to sea on a mission. After years of grieving for him she becomes betrothed to the evil Prince Humperdinck (Chris Sarandon) who masterminds her kidnapping to strengthen his own position in the kingdom.

First off, Westley must defeat a trio of kidnappers headed by the diminutive, but slimy, Wallace Shawn. His accomplices are the kind-hearted giant Fezzik (Andre The Giant) and Inigo Montoya, a Spanish warrior (Mandy Patinkin) out to avenge the murder of his father.

Patinkin's performance especially is a joy to watch and the film comes to life when his longhaired, scruffy cavalier is on screen.

Q — THE WINGED SERPENT

1982, 92 mins, ◇ Ⓥ   *Dir* Larry Cohen   US

★ **Stars** Michael Moriarty, David Carradine, Candy Clark, Richard Roundtree, Malachi McCourt

Q – The Winged Serpent is a delightful science-fiction winner. Larry Cohen's tale of a religious bird of prey terrorizing New York City has wit, style and an above average script for the genre.

Story centers on Michael Moriarty, an ex-junkie who drives getaway cars for the mob. He takes refuge in the Chrysler Building's summit, where he stumbles onto the title character's lair complete with a large unhatched egg.

In the meantime, the green bird has been having a merry feed of workmen and apartment dwellers in the city's high rises. Policeman David Carradine links the arrival of the monster to a series of bizarre ritual killings where the victims are literally skinned alive.

The Winged Serpent has great fun mixing realistic settings with political satire and a wild yarn. Writer-director Cohen has a bagful of tricks and a wild sense of the bizarre to lend the project.

The picture belongs to the bird and Moriarty, and the latter assays his loser with relish.

QUATERMASS AND THE PIT

1968, 98 mins, ◇ *Dir* Roy Ward Baker   UK

★ **Stars** James Donald, Barbara Kelly, Andrew Keir, Julian Glover, Maurice Good, James Culliford, Duncan Lamont

A long-dormant tribe from Mars, accidentally liberated by a London excavation, forms a good story peg for a science-fiction tale.

Nigel Kneale's original script again turns on the Prof. Quatermass character, essayed by Andrew Keir, this time embroiled with a stuffy Colonel Julian Glover when scientist James Donald discovers skeletons in a London subway expansion. Evil demons, brain waves, and sketchy visions of a dying Mars civilization, plus some great special effects work

Andrew Keir and James Donald remove the decaying alien from its underground tomb in **Quatermass and the Pit.**

(considering the obvious budget allocation), provide plot complications.

Given predictable science-versus-military conflicts, and the introduction of Barbara Kelly as a female scientist, film manages to retain interest through suspenseful (if not always clear) exposition of the mysterious creatures.

THE QUATERMASS EXPERIMENT

1955, 81 mins, ▼ *Dir* Val Guest   UK

★ **Stars** Brian Donlevy, Jack Warner, Richard Wordsworth, David King-Wood, Gordon Jackson, Lionel Jeffries

Taken from a BBC television play, *The Quatermass Experiment* is an extravagant piece of science-fiction, based on the after-effects of an assault on space by a rocket ship. Despite its obvious horror angles, production is crammed with incident and suspense.

Brian Donlevy (in the title role) is the scientist who designs a new rocket that is sent hurtling into space with three men on board. It crash-lands in a small English village, with only one survivor. The mystery is what happened to the other two who have disappeared without trace although the rocket ship remained air sealed.

This is unrelieved melodrama. It draws its entertainment from a series of wildly improbable happenings. There

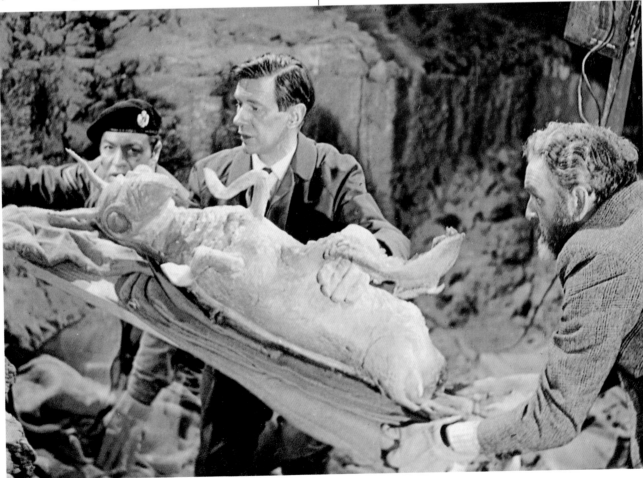

is an occasional over-plus of horror closeups of the victims.

Donlevy plays the part of the scientist with a grim and ruthless conviction.

QUEEN OF OUTER SPACE

1958, 80 mins, ◇ *Dir* Edward Bernds   US

★ *Stars* Zsa Zsa Gabor, Eric Fleming, Laurie Mitchell, Paul Birch, Patrick Waltz, Barbara Darrow

Most of the female characters in *Queen of Outer Space* look like they would be more at home on a Minsky runway than the Cape Canaveral launching pad, but Ben Schwalb's production [based on a story by Ben Hecht] is a good-natured attempt to put some honest sex into science-fiction.

The year is 1985, and Eric Fleming, Patrick Waltz and Dave Willock are US officers in charge of a space ship assigned to check on an American satellite space station. They are deflected from their course by mysterious energy rays from the planet Venus, where their ship is eventually wrecked. Taken prisoner by a malignant queen (Laurie Mitchell), they are about to be destroyed, when they are rescued by a pro-masculine group headed by Zsa Zsa Gabor.

The cast is predominantly feminine and attractively garbed in the brief raiment that appears to be customary on other planets. Gabor makes a handsome leading lady, ro-

manced by Fleming, and the others lend the necessary ingredients to their roles.

QUINTET

1979, 100 mins, ◇ ▼ *Dir* Robert Altman   US

★ *Stars* Paul Newman, Vittorio Gassman, Fernando Rey, Bibi Andersson, Brigitte Fossey, Nina Van Pallandt

Here's another one for Robert Altman's inner circle.

In one of the few obvious points about the picture [based on a story by Altman, Lionel Chetwynd and Patricia Resnick], the title refers to a game popular in some future city (Montreal?) that's slowly dying in a new Ice Age. Though the finer details are anybody's guess, the game involves five players trying to eliminate each other, plus a sixth who comes late to the board.

Paul Newman arrives in the city with his young pregnant bride (Brigitte Fossey) and finds some of the citizens playing the game for real, with Fernando Rey as referee. After losing his bride to a bomb, Newman himself is drawn into the game.

Zsa Zsa Gabor sports an exotic line in extra-terrestrial fashion as she outmanoeuvres **The Queen of Outer Space.**

Global cooling rather than warming provides the chilly setting for Robert Altman's Quintet.

Before it's all over, there have been two bloody throat slashings, a hand bursting open in a fire and one very vigorous stabbing.

RATBOY

1986, 104 mins, ◇ Ⓥ *Dir* Sondra Locke   US

★ **Stars** Sondra Locke, Robert Townsend, Christopher Hewett, Larry Hankin, Sydney Lassick, Gerrit Graham

Yet another picture about how a semi-human, quasi-alien being just can't fit in among earthlings, *Ratboy* can boast of some modest virtues, but is simply too mild on all counts to carry much impact. Oddball first feature from Sondra Locke, who also stars as an out-of-work journalist, deals with eccentric, desperate individuals but in a rather straightforward, unobsessed manner.

The origins of the title character are never investigated or explained. Indeed, after the terrified little bugger is trapped by some transients, he is just blithely manipulated and used by a succession of hustlers who can't put their greed and self-interests on hold long enough to even inquire where the tiny one came from or how he got that way.

Acting tends to the broad side, and Ratboy's nose twitching is cute.

RED PLANET MARS

1952, 87 mins, *Dir* Harry Horner   US

★ **Stars** Peter Graves, Andrea King, Orley Lindgren, Bayard Veiller, Walter Sande, Marvin Miller

Despite its title, *Red Planet Mars* takes place on terra firma, sans space ships, cosmic rays or space cadets. It is a fantastic concoction delving into the realms of science, politics, religion, world affairs and Communism.

Pic's main theme deals with a scientist (Peter Graves) who has managed to achieve radio contact with Mars. Messages from the planet cause all sorts of havoc on earth. The Martians, it appears, have prolonged the life span to 300 years and use cosmic power for energy. As a result of this news and the contact with Mars, mere earth dwellers fear that these secrets will soon be forwarded to earth and will change the entire economic structure of the globe.

Despite the hokum dished out, the actors concerned turn in creditable performances.

RETURN FROM WITCH MOUNTAIN

1978, 93 mins, ◇ Ⓥ *Dir* John Hough US

★ *Stars* Bette Davis, Christopher Lee, Kim Richards, Ike Eisenmann, Jack Soo, Anthony James

Kim Richards and Ike Eisenmann reprise their roles from *Escape to Witch Mountain* (1975) as sister and brother from another world, this time back on Earth for a vacation, courtesy of space traveler Uncle Bene (Denver Pyle). Siblings get a quick test of their psychic powers as mad scientist Christopher Lee and accomplice Bette Davis are testing their mind-control device on henchman Anthony James – when Eisenmann saves James from falling off a building by anti-gravity display, Lee sees the youngster as his meal ticket to world power.

Film is basically a chase caper, as Richards tries to find her brother, aided by a junior bunch of Dead End kids, Christian Juttner, Brad Savage, Poindexter and Jeffrey Jacquet. Despite an extrasensory link between the siblings (they communicate via telepathy, and can also make objects move at will), Lee has Eisenmann strait-jacketed with his device, so he can use youngster's 'molecular reorganization' powers to his own purposes.

RETURN OF THE JEDI

1983, 133 mins, ◇ Ⓥ *Dir* Richard Marquand US

★ *Stars* Mark Hamill, Harrison Ford, Carrie Fisher, Billy Dee Williams, Anthony Daniels, Peter Mayhew

Jedi is the conclusion of the middle trilogy of George Lucas' planned nine-parter and suffers a lot in comparison to the initial *Star Wars* [1977], when all was fresh. One of the apparent problems is neither the writers nor the principal performers are putting in the same effort.

Telegraphed in the preceding *The Empire Strikes Back* [1980], the basic dramatic hook this time is Mark Hamill's quest to discover – and do something about – the true identity of menacing Darth Vader, while resisting the evil intents of the Emperor (Ian McDiarmid).

Hamill is not enough of a dramatic actor to carry the plot load here, especially when his partner in so many

scenes is really little more than an oversized gas pump, even if splendidly voiced by James Earl Jones.

Even worse, Harrison Ford, who was such an essential element of the first two outings, is present more in body than in spirit this time, given little to do but react to special effects. And it can't be said that either Carrie Fisher or Billy Dee Williams rise to previous efforts.

But Lucas and director Richard Marquand have overwhelmed these performer flaws with a truly amazing array of creatures, old and new, plus the familiar space hardware.

ROBOCOP

1987, 103 mins, ◇ Ⓥ *Dir* Paul Verhoeven US

★ *Stars* Peter Weller, Nancy Allen, Ronny Cox, Kurtwood Smith

RoboCop is a comic book movie that's definitely not for kids. The welding of extreme violence with four-letter words is tempered with gut-level humor and technical wizardry.

Roller-coaster ride begins with the near-dismemberment of recently transferred police officer Murphy (Peter Weller), to the southern precinct of the Detroit Police Dept in the not-too-distant future.

There are three organizations inextricably wound into Detroit's anarchical society – the police, a band of sadistic hoodlums, and a multinational conglomerate which has a contract with the city to run the police force.

Weller is blown to bits just at the time an ambitious junior exec at the multinational is ready to develop a prototype cyborg – half-man, half-machine programmed to be an indestructable cop. Thus Weller becomes RoboCop, unleashed to fell the human scum he encounters, not the least among them his killers.

As sicko sadists go, Kurtwood Smith is a well-cast adversary. Nancy Allen as Weller's partner (before he died) provides the only warmth in the film, wanting and encouraging RoboCop to listen to some of the human spirit that survived inside him. *RoboCop* is as tightly worked as a film can be, not a moment or line wasted.

ROBOCOP 2

1990, 118 mins, ◇ Ⓥ *Dir* Irvin Kershner US

★ *Stars* Peter Weller, Nancy Allen, Dan O'Herlihy, Belinda Bauer, Tom Noonan, Galyn Gorg

This ultraviolent, nihilistic sequel has enough technical dazzle to impress hardware fans, but obviously no one in the Orion front office told filmmakers that less is more.

The future is represented by a crumbling Detroit (actually filmed like the original in Texas), dominated by Dan O'Herlihy's Omni Consumer Products company. He's set to foreclose on loans and literally take possession of Motown. Standing in his way is a loose cannon, drug

The Millenium Falcon followed by fighters of the Rebel Alliance attack the Death Star in Return of the Jedi.

magnate/user Tom Noonan, whose goal is to flood society with designer versions of his drug Nuke.

Peter Weller as RoboCop must defeat both factions while effeminate mayor Willard Pugh gets in the way. Noonan is reconstituted as Robocop 2 by O'Herlihy's sexy assistant Belinda Bauer, providing the film's final half hour of great special effects as an end in themselves.

Gabriel Damon as a precocious 12-year-old gangster is the best thing in the picture.

ROBOT MONSTER

1953, 62 mins, ⊗ *Dir* Phil Tucker   US

★ *Stars* George Nader, Claudia Barrett, Selena Royle, Gregory Moffett, John Mylong, Pamela Paulson

Judged on the basis of novelty, as a showcase for the Tru-Stereo Process, *Robot Monster* comes off surprisingly well, considering the extremely limited budget ($50,000) and schedule on which the film was shot.

The Tru-Stereo Process (3-D) utilized here is easy on the eyes, coming across clearly at all times. To the picture's credit no 3-D gimmicks were employed.

Beating Arch Oboler's *Five* [1951] by one survivor, yarn here concerns itself with the last six people on earth – all pitted against a mechanical monster called Ro-Man, sent from another planet whose 'people' are disturbed by strides being made on earth in the research fields of atomic development and space travel.

Sextet – a famed scientist, his wife, assistant, daughter and two children – are protected from Ro-Man's supersonic death ray by anti-biotic serum.

Of the principals, George Nader, as the aide who falls in love with and eventually marries the scientist's daughter in a primitive ceremony, fares the best. Selena Royle also comes across okay, but of the others the less said the better.

THE ROCKETEER

1991, 108 mins, ◇ ⊗ *Dir* Joe Johnston   US

★ *Stars* Bill Campbell, Jennifer Connelly, Alan Arkin, Timothy Dalton, Paul Sorvino, Ed Lauter

Based on a comic ['graphic novel' by Dave Stevens] unveiled in 1981, this $40 million adventure fantasy puts a shiny polish on familiar elements: airborne hero, damsel in distress, Nazi villains, 1930s Hollywood glamor, dazzling special effects.

Rocketeer's elaborate opening sequence has an ace pilot (Bill Campbell) testing a new racing aeroplane over Las Angeles skies in 1938 while, down on the ground below, hoods and Feds in speeding cars shoot it out after the rob-

EXCLUSIVE FILMS *presents*

GEORGE NADER · **CLAUDIA BARRETT**

in

ROBOT MONSTER Ⓤ

with SELENA ROYLE · GREGORY MOFFETT · PAMELA DAWSON

Above: *George Nader protests in vain as the* **Robot Monster** *carries off the heroine in traditional style.*

bery of some mysterious device.

Developed by none other than Howard Hughes, the invention makes its way into the ace pilot's hands, but it's coveted by a dashing star of swashbuckling adventure films who also happens to be a dedicated Nazi (Timothy Dalton). Although he has hired thugs led by Paul Sorvino to recover the priceless device, Dalton has his own ideas about getting at Campbell through his gorgeous girlfriend (played by Jennifer Connelly).

The object of intense interest is a portable rocket pack which, if strapped to one's back, can send its wearer zipping around almost as fast, if not as quietly, as Superman.

Newcomer Campbell exhibits the requisite grit and all-American know-how, but the lead role is written with virtually no humor or subtext. Those around him come off to better advantage, notably Dalton as the deliciously smooth, insidious Sinclair; Sorvino and Alan Arkin, with the latter as the Rocketeer's mentor; Terry O'Quinn as Hughes; and the lovely, voluptuous Connelly.

Left: *Peter Weller as Robocop and Nancy Allen as his human partner patrol the streets of Detroit in* **Robocop 2.**

ROLLERBALL

•1975, 129 mins, ◇ *Dir* Norman Jewison   US

★ *Stars* James Caan, John Houseman, Maud Adams, John Beck, Moses Gunn, Pamela Hensley

Norman Jewison's sensational futuristic drama about a world of Corporate States stars James Caan in an excellent performance as a famed athlete who fights for his identity and free will. The $5 million film was made in Munich and London.

The year is 2018, and the world has been regrouped politically to a hegemony of six conglomerate cartels. There is total material tranquility: no wars, no poverty, no unrest – and no personal free will and no God.

The ingenious way of ventilating human nature's animal-violence residual content is the world sport of rollerball, a combination of roller derby, motorcycle racing and basketball where violent death is part of the entertainment. Caan is a long-standing hero of the sport, becoming dangerously popular. He is ordered to retire. He refuses. Tilt.

The very fine music track was supervised and conducted by Andre Previn, utilizing excerpts from Bach, Shostakovich, Tschaikovsky and Albinoni / Giazotto, plus

Futuristic gladiators clash in the often-lethal spectator 'sport' of **Rollerball.**

original Previn work which included the corporate anthems which begin each game.

The performances of the principals are uniformly tops. Besides the great work of Caan, John Houseman and Ralph Richardson, John (as head of the corporation) Beck is excellent as the model yahoo jock. As the women in Caan's life, Maud Adams, Pamela Hensley and Barbara Trentham step right out of today's deodorant and cosmetics teleblurbs – just the way they're supposed to be when life imitates consumer advertising imagery.

RUNAWAY

1982, 100 mins, ◇ ⓥ *Dir* Michael Crichton   US

★ *Stars* Tom Selleck, Cynthia Rhodes, Gene Simmons, Kirstie Alley, Stan Shaw, Joey Cramer

Tom Selleck, with a cop's short haircut and playing a workaday stiff who's afraid of heights, cuts a less dashing but more accessible figure in *Runaway* than in prior pictures. However, this Michael Crichton robotic nightmare is so trite that the story seems lifted from Marvel Comics, with heat-seeking bullets and a villain so bad he would be fun if the film wasn't telling us to take this near futuristic adventure with a straight face.

Selleck's fem police partner Cynthia Rhodes is all overachiever and formula romantic foil to Selleck, who's single parent raising a son. Departure may be fresh for Selleck but the comparative lack of his trademarked sardonic humor does cost the pic.

THE RUNNING MAN

1987, 101 mins, ◇ ⓥ *Dir* Paul Michael Glaser   US

★ *Stars* Arnold Schwarzenegger, Maria Conchita Alonso, Richard Dawson, Yaphet Kotto, Jim Brown, Jesse Ventura

Pic, based on a novel by Richard Bachman (Stephen King), opens in 2017 when the world, following a financial collapse, is run by a police state, with TV a heavily censored propaganda tool of the government. Arnold Schwarzenegger is Ben Richards, a helicopter pilot who disobeys orders to fire on unarmed people during an LA food riot. He's

Tom Selleck tries to keep away from the deadly robotic 'spiders' in **Runaway.**

slapped in prison and escapes 18 months later with pals Yaphet Kotto and Marvin J. McIntyre.

Producer-host of the popular TV gameshow *The Running Man* Damon Killian (Richard Dawson) orders Richards up as his next contestant and he is duly captured and made a runner in this lethal (and fixed) gladiatorial contest for the masses.

Format works only on a pure action level, with some exciting, but overly repetitive, roller-coaster style sequences of runners hurtling into the game through tunnels on futuristic sleds. Bloated budget was $27 million.

Schwarzenegger sadistically dispatches the baddies, enunciating typical wisecrack remarks (many repeated from his previous films), but it's all too easy, despite the casting of such powerful presences as Jim Brown and former wrestlers Jesse Ventura and Prof Toru Tanaka.

SATURN 3

1980, 88 mins, ◇ Ⓥ *Dir* Stanley Donen   UK

★ *Stars* Farrah Fawcett, Kirk Douglas, Harvey Keitel, Ed Bishop

Somewhere in deepest, darkest space, Kirk Douglas and Farrah Fawcett jog around through a space station that looks suspiciously like Bloomingdale's after closing. The pair are scientists doing important work, when bad guy Harvey Keitel shows up.

A gladiatorial-style gameshow has Arnold Schwarzenegger playing for ultimate odds in **The Running Man.**

Douglas is sprightly, but he has to handle some pretty awful lines in this Martin Amis script [from a story by John Barry]. Keitel's dialog, if quoted, would be on a par.

Life goes on in this shopping mall of lights till Keitel builds Hector, the mad robot, whose tubes and hubcaps develop goosebumps for Farrah.

Best scene in the entire effort is Hector's resurrection after he has been dismantled for being randy. The parts find each other and reconnect which is more than this film does.

SAVAGES

1972, 105 mins, ◇ Ⓥ *Dir* James Ivory   US

★ *Stars* Louis J. Stadlen, Anne Francine, Thayer David, Susan Blakely, Russ Thacker, Salome Jens

Savages, first US film by producer Ismail Merchant and director James Ivory, is about members of a primitive tribe who are lured by the appearance of a rolling croquet ball to an old deserted mansion where they dress in clothes and take on 'civilized' societal behavior, only to return to the forest and their primitive behavior the following morning. The playing has flair and grace, sans woodenness from everyone, with Walter Lassally's excellently balanced b&w lensing for the primitive days and color for the so-called civilized times a great asset, as are the editing and music. The only carp might be a tendency to overplay an act.

But no denying an almost hypnotic charm and fascination in this offbeat, insouciant look at mankind and his climb to civilization and fall.

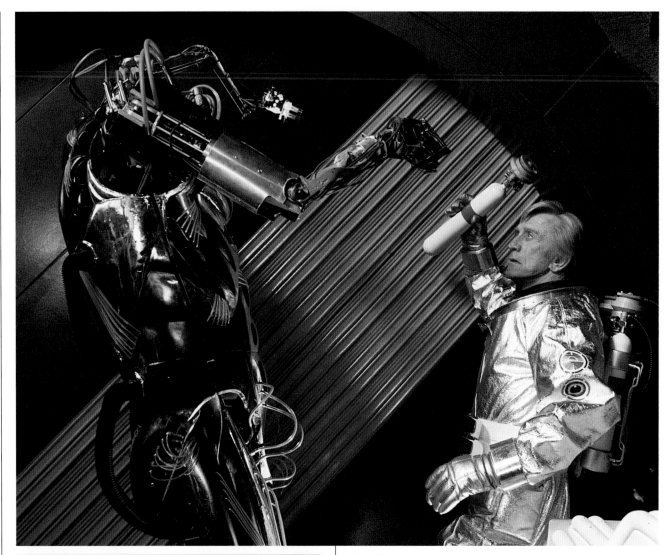

*Kirk Douglas spars with Hector the rampant robot in the space station actioner **Saturn 3**.*

SECONDS

1966, 108 mins, ◇ *Dir* John Frankenheimer   US

★ *Stars* Rock Hudson, Salome Jens, John Randolph, Will Geer, Jeff Corey, Richard Anderson

US suburbia boredom is treated in an original manner in this cross between a sci-fi opus, a thriller, a suspense pic and a parable on certain aspects of American middle-class life.

A middle-aged man has lost contact with his wife. His only daughter is married and gone. Even his work, which was once his mainstay in life, seems to pall. Into this comes a strange call from a supposedly dead friend to come to a certain place.

He finds himself in a mysterious big business surgery corporation with some disquieting features of a room full of listless men. He is told he can be redone surgically to become a young man and start life over again. He decides to go through with it and after surgery wakes up as Rock Hudson.

This has some intriguing aspects on the yearning for youth and a chance to live life over again by many men. But this Faustian theme is barely touched on and the hero's tie with the past is also somewhat arbitrary. Film [from the novel by David Ely] does not quite come off as a thriller, sci-fi adjunct or philosophical fable.

THE 7TH VOYAGE OF SINBAD

1958, 89 mins, ◇ ▼ *Dir* Nathan Juran   UK

★ *Stars* Kerwin Mathews, Kathryn Grant, Richard Eyer, Torin Thatcher, Alec Mango, Danny Green

Just about every trick in the book – including one called Dynamation, i.e. the animation of assorted monsters, vultures, skeletons, etc – has been used to bring a vivid sort of realism to the serious and terrifying hazards which Sinbad encounters on his voyage and in his battle with Sokurah the magician. Add to this a love story, interrupted when the princess Parisa is shrunk to inch-size by the magician, and what emerges is a bright, noisy package.

S

Kerwin Matthews makes a pleasant Sinbad, acting the part with more restraint than bravura; Kathryn Grant is pretty as the princess; Torin Thatcher has a fittingly evil look as the magician; Richard Eyer is cute as the genie; and Alec Mango has dignity as the Caliph.

But this isn't the sort of film in which performances matter much. It's primarily entertainment for the eye, and the action moves swiftly and almost without interruption. Ray Harryhausen, who was responsible for visual effects, emerges as the hero of this piece.

SHORT CIRCUIT

1986, 98 mins, ◇ Ⓥ   *Dir* John Badham   US

★ *Stars* Ally Sheedy, Steve Guttenberg, Fisher Stevens, Austin Pendleton, G.W. Bailey, Brian McNamara

Short Circuit is a hip, sexless sci-fi sendup featuring a Defense Dept robot who comes 'alive' to become a pop-talking peacenik.

Robot is the one-dimensional No. 5, the ultimate weapon designed by playful computer whiz Dr Newton Crosby (Steve Guttenberg).

The 'Lord of the Flys' theme of Savages sees the noble primitives descending to the level of so-called civilization.

By a fluke, No. 5 gets short-circuited and begins to malfunction. It finds itself outside the high-security Nova compound in a chase that lands it on top of a natural foods catering truck and under the influence of its sweet but tough animal-loving owner, Stephanie (Ally Sheedy). Scripters get credit for some terrific dialog that would have been a lot less disarming if not for the winsome robot and Sheedy's affection for it. Guttenberg plays his best goofy self.

SHORT CIRCUIT 2

1988, 110 mins, ◇ Ⓥ   *Dir* Kenneth Johnson   US

★ *Stars* Fisher Stevens, Michael McLean, Cynthia Gibb, Jack Weston, Dee McCafferty

Mild and meek, *Short Circuit 2* has an uncomplicated sweetness as a successful followup to the original robot kiddie comedy.

'Johnny Five' makes his way to the Big City, where

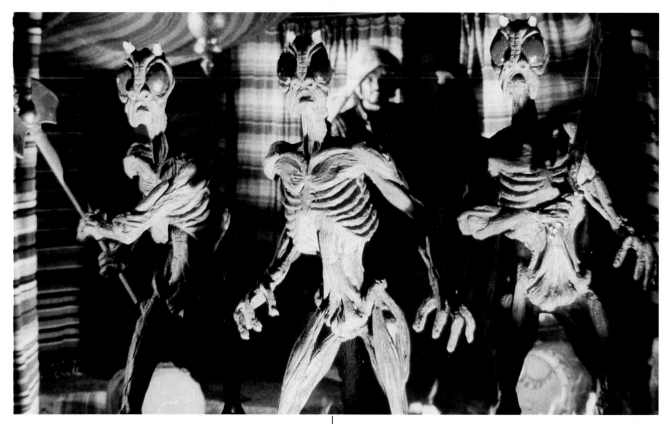

protector Fisher Stevens struggles to make ends meet hawking toy models of his mechanical wonder on the street.

Cutie-pie store employee Cynthia Gibb needs to bring a novel item to her shelves, and sends Stevens and self-styled entrepreneur Michael McKean into instant action by ordering 1,000 of the little buggers for the Christmas season. Underhanded banker Jack Weston has some other ideas for the tireless automaton, scheming to kidnap it and press it into service stealing some priceless jewels from a safe deposit box.

Although derivative, the robot, made up of all manner of spare electronic parts, remains charming, and kids will undoubtedly find delightful scenes in which Number Five jumps around from place to place and sails through the air amid the skyscrapers of Toronto.

The film is set in a generic US metropolis, complete with American flags and a citizenship swearing-in ceremony. However, the city is constantly recognizable as Toronto.

SILENT RUNNING

1972, 89 mins, ◇ Ⓥ   *Dir* Douglas Trumbull   US

★ **Stars** Bruce Dern, Cliff Potts, Ron Rifkin, Jesse Vint

Silent Running depends on the excellent special effects of debuting director Douglas Trumbull and his team and on the appreciation of a literate but broadly entertaining script. Those being the highlights, they are virtually wiped out by the crucial miscasting of Bruce Dern. As a result, the production lacks much dramatic credibility and often teeters on the edge of the ludicrous.

Dern and three clod companions man a space vehicle

The 7th Voyage of Sinbad *has hokum aplenty as everything is pulled out of the fx cupboard – even the skeletons.*

in a fleet of airships containing vegetation in case the earth again can support that type of life. But the program is scuttled, all hands are recalled, but Dern decides to mutiny. In the process, he kills his three shipmates and goes deeper into space. His only companions are two small robots, whose life-like qualities are rather touching.

SINBAD AND THE EYE OF THE TIGER

1977, 112 mins, ◇ Ⓥ   *Dir* Sam Wanamaker   US

★ **Stars** Patrick Wayne, Taryn Power, Margaret Whiting, Jane Seymour, Patrick Troughton, Kurt Christian

The plot takes Patrick Wayne, as Sinbad, on a quest to free a prince (Damien Thomas) from the spell of evil sorceress Margaret Whiting. Thomas has quite a dilemma, in that he's turned into a baboon and is fast losing all vestiges of human behavior. Along for the odyssey are a couple of young cuties (Taryn Power and Jane Seymour) who keep their modest demeanor while wearing scanty outfits.

The plot scenes are hammy beyond belief. Whiting is a particular offender with her all-stops-out villainy. When the fantasy creatures have center stage, the film is enjoyable to watch. Such beasties as skeletons, a giant bee and an outsized walrus, are marvelously vivified by Ray Harryhausen. Most of the studio work was done in England, with locations in Spain, Malta, and the Mediterranean.

SLAUGHTERHOUSE-FIVE

1972, 104 mins, ◇ Ⓥ *Dir* George Roy Hill   US

★ *Stars* Michael Sacks, Ron Leibman, Eugene Roche, Sharon Gans, Valerie Perrine, Roberts Blossom

Slaughterhouse-Five is a mechanically slick, dramatically sterile commentary about World War II and afterward, as seen through the eyes of a boob Everyman. Director George Roy Hill's arch achievement emphasizes the diffused cant to the detriment of characterizations, which are stiff, unsympathetic and skin-deep.

Stephen Geller's adaptation of Kurt Vonnegut Jr's novel *Slaughterhouse-Five or The Children's Crusade* is in an academic sense fluid and lucid. Michael Sacks in his screen debut plays Billy Pilgrim, the luckless loser who always seems to be in the wrong place at the wrong time.

The story jumps around from its beginning in World War II where as a dumb draftee Pilgrim becomes a prisoner of war in Germany.

In the postwar period, Pilgrim moves into the orbits of overweight wife and predictable offspring.

Lost in space: Bruce Dern and automaton friends try to figure out their future in **Silent Running.**

SLIPSTREAM

1989, 101 mins, ◇ Ⓥ *Dir* Steven Lisberger   UK

★ *Stars* Mark Hamill, Bob Peck, Bill Paxton, Kitty Aldridge, Ben Kingsley, F. Murray Abraham

British-made sci-fi adventure romp *Slipstream* is one of those films that had potential, but unfortunately it doesn't make the grade.

Slipstream seems to be making some kind of ecological message; the film's version of Earth [from a story by Sam Clemens] is a place ruined by pollution with the planet washed clean by a river of wind called the 'Slipstream.'

Lawman Mark Hamill and his partner Kitty Aldridge capture Bob Peck, who's wanted for murder. When adventurer Bill Paxton discovers there is a price on Peck's head he snatches him and makes his escape down the Slipstream.

They come across a cult of religious fanatics who worship the wind, led by Ben Kingsley. A member of the cult (Eleanor David) falls for Peck – even though it turns out he is an android.

The strong points are the stunning locations (Turkey and the Yorkshire moors), the performances by Hamill and Aldridge, plus impressive aircraft and technical effects. Kingsley and F. Murray Abraham have virtual walk-on parts.

S

SOMETHING WICKED THIS WAY COMES

1983, 94 mins, ◇ Ⓥ *Dir* Jack Clayton   US

★ *Stars* Jason Robards, Jonathan Pryce, Diane Ladd, Pam Grier, Royal Dano, Vidal Peterson

Film version of Ray Bradbury's popular novel is something of a disappointment. Possibilities for a dark, child's view fantasy set in rural America of yore are visible throughout the $20 million production but various elements have not entirely congealed into a unified achievement.

Location scenes shot in an astonishingly beautiful Vermont autumn stand in for early 20th-century Illinois, where two young boys are intrigued by the untimely arrival of a mysterious carnival troupe. By day, fairgrounds seem innocent enough, but by night they possess a strange allure which leads local inhabitants to fall victim to their deepest desires.

Thanks to the diabolical talents of carnival leader Mr Dark, played by the suitably sinister Jonathan Pryce, these wishes can be granted, but at the price of becoming a member of the traveling freak show. Mr Dark decides that little Will and Jim would make excellent recruits and pursues them vigilantly until the apocalyptic finale.

SOMEWHERE IN TIME

1980, 103 mins, ◇ Ⓥ *Dir* Jeannot Szwarc   US

★ *Stars* Christopher Reeve, Jane Seymour, Christopher Plummer, Teresa Wright, Bill Erwin, Sean Hayden

A charming, witty, passionate romantic drama about a love transcending space and time, *Somewhere In Time* is an old-fashioned film in the best sense of that term. Which means it's carefully crafted, civilized in its sensibilities, and interested more in characterization than in shock effects.

Christopher Reeve is a young Chicago playwright who becomes mysteriously fascinated by a 1912 photo of a stage actress (Jane Seymour).

Reeve is drawn to a hotel on Mackinac Island in Michigan, where it transpires they actually did meet and have an affair at the time the photo was taken.

Seymour is lovely and mesmerizing enough to justify Reeve's grand romantic obsession with her.

THE SON OF KONG

1933, 69 mins, *Dir* Ernest B. Schoedsack   US

★ *Stars* Robert Armstrong, Helen Mack, Frank Reicher, John Marston, Victor Wong, Lee Kohlmar

This is the sequel to and wash-up of the King Kong theme, consisting of salvaged remnants from the original production and rating as fair entertainment.

Story is by Ruth Rose who, with, others, worked on the adaptation of the original. It is concerned mostly in building up the explorer's return to the island of prehistoric animals, which cuts down the actual running time of the trick stuff to perhaps less than 25% of the total footage.

His pop was one tough hombre, but young Kong is lots more friendly. The explorer saves him from destruction in quicksand, so he proceeds to reciprocate. He wrassles and kayoes some bad eggs among the beasts of the stone age jungle while protecting the visiting mortals. The senior Kong was around 50 feet high in his bare tootsies. Junior is a comparative shrimp, standing a mere 25 feet or so, but he can handle himself in a scrap.

Three of the principals, Robert Armstrong, Frank Reicher and Victor Wong, are holdovers from the original cast. Helen Mack is the girl this time, called upon to be a brave creature, in place of Fay Wray who was directed into doing nothing but screaming.

SOYLENT GREEN

1973, 97 mins, ◇ Ⓥ *Dir* Richard Fleischer   US

★ *Stars* Charlton Heston, Leigh Taylor-Young, Chuck Connors, Joseph Cotten, Brock Peters, Edward G. Robinson

The somewhat plausible and proximate horrors in the story of *Soylent Green* carry the production over its awkward spots to the status of a good futuristic exploitation film.

The year is 2022, the setting NY City, where millions of over-populated residents exist in a smog-insulated police state, where the authorities wear strange-looking foreign uniforms (not the gray flannel suits which is more likely the case), and where real food is a luxury item. Charlton Heston is a detective assigned to the assassination murder of industrialist Joseph Cotten, who has discovered the shocking fact that the Soylent Corp, of which he is a director, is no longer capable of making synthetic food from the dying sea. The substitute – the reconstituted bodies of the dead.

The character Heston plays is pivotal, since he is supposed to be the prototype average man of the future who really swallows whole the social system. Edward G. Robinson, his investigative aide, reminisces about the old days – green fields, flowers, natural food, etc. But the script bungles seriously by confining Heston's outrage to the secret of Soylent Green.

SPACEBALLS

1987, 96 mins, ◇ Ⓥ *Dir* Mel Brooks   US

★ *Stars* Mel Brooks, John Candy, Rick Moranis, Bill Pullman, Daphne Zuniga

Mel Brooks will do anything for a laugh. Unfortunately, what he does in *Spaceballs*, a misguided parody of the *Star Wars* adventures, isn't very funny.

Pic features Bill Pullman as Lone Starr and Daphne

Zuniga as Princess Vespa, former a composite of Harrison Ford and Mark Hamill, latter a Carrie Fisher clone. Pullman's partner is John Candy as Barf, a half-man, half-dog creature who is his own best friend. Equipped with a constantly wagging tale and furry sneakers, Barf is one of the better comic creations here.

The plot about the ruthless race of Spaceballs out to steal the air supply from the planet Druidia is more clichd than the original. Brooks turns up in the dual role of President Skroob of Spaceballs and the all-knowing, all-powerful Yogurt.

Brooks' direction is far too static to suggest the sweeping style of the *Star Wars* epics and pic more closely resembles Flash Gordon programmers. Aside from a few isolated laughs *Spaceballs* is strictly not kosher.

SPACECAMP

1986, 107 mins, ◇ ⊛   *Dir* Harry Winer   US

★ *Stars* Kate Capshaw, Lea Thompson, Kelly Preston, Larry B. Scott, Leaf Phoenix, Tate Donovan

SpaceCamp is a youthful view of outer space set at the real-life United States Space Camp in Huntsville, Alabama for aspiring young astronauts. Pic never successfully integrates summer camp hijinks with outer space idealism to come up with a dramatically compelling story.

Hampered by cliche-ridden dialog, performances suffer from a weightlessness of their own. Kate Capshaw as the instructor and one trained astronaut to make the flight neither looks nor acts the part of a serious scientist.

As for the kids, Tate Donovan as the shuttle commander-in-training is uninteresting and Lea Thompson as his would-be girlfriend is too young and naive for words, even the ones she's given.

SPACEHUNTER: ADVENTURES IN THE FORBIDDEN ZONE

1983, 90 mins, ◇ ⊚   *Dir* Lamont Johnson   US

★ *Stars* Peter Strauss, Molly Ringwald, Ernie Hudson, Andrea Marcovicci, Michael Ironside, Beeson Carroll

Spacehunter is muddied 3-D action set in the mid-21st Century on the planet Terra Eleven of a double-star system

Ernie Hudson, Molly Ringwald and Peter Strauss on the rescue trail in Spacehunter: Adventures in the Forbidden Zone.

where an Earth colony has been reduced to 'Road Warrior'-style rubble by wars and plague.

Weak story premise has salvage ship pilot Wolff (Peter Strauss) and other 'Earthers', including orphaned waif Niki (Molly Ringwald) and Washington (Ernie Hudson) searching the planet for three shipwrecked, later kidnapped girls.

Episodic treatment pits them against local dangers, including a well-executed set of puffy monsters, en route to showdown of tryant McNabb known as Overdog (Michael Ironside).

Aside from fine stuntwork in an early battle involving a vast sail-riged galleon running on railroad tracks and the impressive depth effects in the final reel, *Spacehunter* is a dull trek picture.

STARMAN

1984, 115 mins, ◇ Ⓥ *Dir* John Carpenter   US

★ *Stars* Jeff Bridges, Karen Allen, Charles Martin Smith, Richard Jaeckel, Robert Phalen, Tony Edwards

There is little that is original in *Starman*, but at least it has chosen good models As amalgam of elements introduced in *Close Encounters of the Third Kind*, *E.T.* and even *The Man Who Fell to Earth*, *Starman* shoots for the miraculous and only partially hits its target.

The Starman (Jeff Bridges) arrives much like 'E.T.' – an alien in a hostile environment – but in an elaborate transformation scene he assumes human form. The body he chooses for his sojourn on Earth happens to belong to the dead husband of Jenny Hayden (Karen Allen) who lives alone in a remote section of Wisconsin.

Bridges and Allen set off on a trip across the country to Arizona where the Starman must make his connection to return home.

STAR TREK THE MOTION PICTURE

1979, 132 mins, ◇ Ⓥ *Dir* Robert Wise   US

★ *Stars* William Shatner, Leonard Nimoy, DeForest Kelley, George Takei, James Doohan, Persis Khambatta

The *Enterprise* has been completely reconditioned during a two-year drydock, but must be prematurely dispatched to intercept an Earth-bound attacker.

William Shatner's Kirk is told to lead the mission along with other show regulars.

Upshot is a search-and-destroy thriller [based on a story by Alan Dean Foster] that includes all of the ingredients the TV show's fans thrive on: the philosophical dilemma

Jeff Bridges' Starman reveals what the future has in hand for Karen Allen before he returns to his home planet.

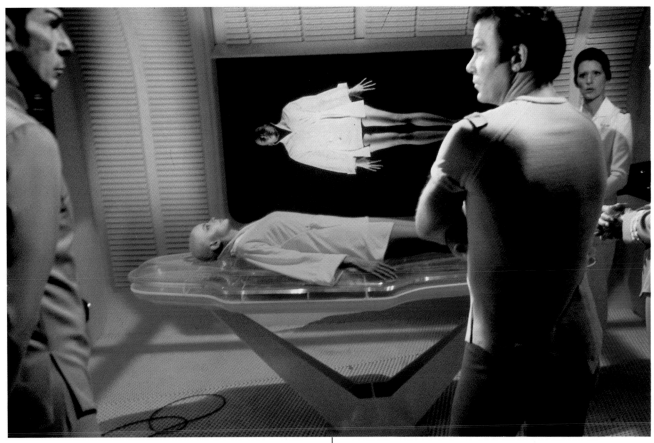

wrapped in a scenario of mind control, troubles with the space ship, the dependable and understanding Kirk, the ever-logical Spock, and suspenseful take with twist ending. Touches of romance and corn also dot this voyage.

But the expensive effects (under supervision of Douglas Trumbull) are the secret of this film, and the amazing wizardry throughout would appear to justify the whopping budget. Jerry Goldsmith's brassy score is the other necessary plus.

STAR TREK II THE WRATH OF KHAN

1982, 113 mins, ◇ Ⓥ *Dir* Nicholas Meyer   US

★ *Stars* William Shatner, Leonard Nimoy, DeForest Kelley, Ricardo Montalban, James Doohan, Walter Koenig

Star Trek II is a very satisfying space adventure, closer in spirit and format to the popular TV series than to its big-budget predecessor.

Story is nominally a sequel to the TV episode *Space Seed*, with Starship Reliant captain Terrell (Paul Winfield) and Commander Chekov (Walter Koenig) incorrectly landing on a planet on an exploration mission. This allows the evil Khan (Ricardo Montalban) who was marooned there with his family and crew 15 years before by Kirk (William Shatner), to take over the Reliant and vow revenge on Kirk.

Admiral Kirk is coaxed to take command once again of the Starship *Enterprise* on a training mission, travels to the Regula space station on a rescue mission. Dr Carol Marcus

Leonard Nimoy, Persis Khambatta and William Shatner take the Enterprise onto the big screen in Star Trek.

(Bibi Besch) and her (and Kirk's) son David (Merritt Butrick) have been working there on the Genesis Project, to convert barren planets into Eden-like sources of life. Khan has stolen the Genesis Effect equipment.

Final reel is a classic of emotional manipulation: Spock unhesitatingly calculates that he must sacrifice himself to save the Enterprise crew.

STAR TREK III THE SEARCH FOR SPOCK

1984, 105 mins, ◇ Ⓥ *Dir* Leonard Nimoy   US

★ *Stars* William Shatner, DeForest Kelley, James Doohan, George Takei, Walter Koenig, Leonard Nimoy

Star Trek III is an emotionally satisfying science-fiction adventure. Dovetailing neatly with the previous entry in the popular series *Star Trek II*, film centers upon a quest to seemingly bring Spock (Leonard Nimoy), the noble science officer and commander who selflessly gave his life to save 'the many', back to life.

Spock's friend, Admiral Kirk (William Shatner) is visited by Spock's Vulcan father (Mark Lenard), who informs him that Spock's living spirit may still be alive via a mindmeld with one of the crew and must be taken to the planet Vulcan to be preserved.

Kirk discovers who the 'possessed' crew member is, and with his other shipmates, steals the Enterprise out of its dock and sets off for Vulcan.

STAR TREK IV THE VOYAGE HOME

1986, 119 mins, ◇ Ⓥ *Dir* Leonard Nimoy   US

★ *Stars* William Shatner, Leonard Nimoy, DeForest Kelley, James Doohan, Catherine Hicks, George Takei

Latest excursion is warmer, wittier, more socially relevant and truer to its TV origins than prior odysseys.

This voyage finds the crew earthbound but they find the galaxy dark and messages from Earth distorted. Spock locates the source of the trouble in the bleating, eerie sounds of an unidentified probe and links them to a cry from the Earth's past that has long been silenced.

Scripters employ successful use of time travel.

Spock (Leonard Nimoy) and Kirk (William Shatner) play off each other in a sort of deadpan futuristic version of Hope and Crosby with Nimoy, surprisingly, as the awkward one relying on Shatner's smooth talking to win the help of a zealous save-the-whales biologist (Catherine Hicks) in capturing a couple of specimens.

STAR TREK V THE FINAL FRONTIER

1989, 106 mins, ◇ Ⓥ *Dir* William Shatner   US

★ *Stars* William Shatner, Leonard Nimoy, DeForest Kelley, James Doohan, Nichelle Nichols, George Takei

Even diehard Trekkies may be disappointed by *Star Trek V.* Coming after Leonard Nimoy's delightful directorial outing on *Star Trek IV*, William Shatner's inauspicious feature directing debut is a double letdown.

A major flaw in the story [by Shatner, Harve Bennett and David Loughery] is that it centers on an obsessive quest by a character who isn't a member of the Enterprise crew, a renegade Vulcan played by Laurence Luckinbill in Kabuki-like makeup. The crazed Luckinbill kidnaps the crew and makes them fly to a never-before-visited planet at the centre of the galaxy in quest of the Meaning of Life.

Better they should have stayed home and watched re-runs of the TV series, which had a lot more to say about the meaning of life.

Shatner, rises to the occasion, however, in directing a dramatic sequence of the mystical Luckinbill teaching Nimoy and DeForest Kelley to re-experience their long-buried traumas. The recreations of Spock's rejection by his father after his birth and Kelley's euthanasia of his own father are moving highlights.

Back to the present, as the Trekkies tread warily through the traffic in Star Trek IV The Voyage Home.

STAR WARS

1977, 121 mins, ◇ Ⓥ *Dir* George Lucas   US

★ *Stars* Mark Hamill, Harrison Ford, Carrie Fisher, Peter Cushing, Alec Guinness, Anthony Daniels

Academy Award: 1977: Best Picture (Nomination)

Star Wars is a magnificent film. George Lucas set out to make the biggest possible adventure fantasy out of his

memories of serials and older action epics, and he succeeded brilliantly.

The superb balance of technology and human drama is one of the many achievements: one identifies with the characters and accepts, as do they, the intriguing intergalactic world in which they live.

Carrie Fisher is delightful as the regal, but spunky princess on a rebel planet who has been kidnapped by Peter Cushing, would-be ruler of the universe. Mark Hamill is excellent as a farm boy who sets out to rescue Fisher in league with Alec Guinness, last survivor of a band of noble knights. Harrison Ford is outstanding, too; as the likable mercenary pilot, Han Solo.

STEPFORD WIVES

1975, 114 mins, ◇ *Dir* Bryan Forbes   US

★ *Stars* Katharine Ross, Paula Prentiss, Peter Masterson, Nanette Newman, Patrick O'Neal, Tina Louise

Bryan Forbes' filmization of Ira Levin's *The Stepford Wives* is a quietly freaky suspense-horror story.

Katharine Ross (in an excellent and assured performance), husband Peter Masterson and kids depart NY's

S

urban pressures to a seemingly bovine Connecticut existence. Trouble is, Ross and new friend Paula Prentiss (also excellent) find all the other wives exuding sticky hairspray homilies and male chauvinist fantasy responses. When Prentiss finally changes her own attitude, Ross panics but cannot escape.

Patrick O'Neal heads a local men's club that somehow is involved in the unseen, sluggishly developed but eventually exciting climax.

The black humor and sophistication of the plot is handled extremely well.

STEREO

1969, 63 mins, *Dir* David Cronenberg   CANADA

★ **Stars** Ron Mlodzik, Jack Messinger, Iain Ewing, Clara Mayer, Paul Mulholland, Arlene Mlodzik

Lensed for a paltry $3,500, *Stereo* is the initial feature film effort by David Cronenberg.

Shot in black-and-white without synch sound, *Stereo* carries built-in liabilities thanks to its technical limitations and aesthetic idiosyncracies. Basically a student effort (Cronenberg was 26), pic tests the viewer's patience and endurance even with its hour's running time due to its emphatically dry, scientific narration and deliberate emotional distancing.

Film abstractly examines the situation at the Canadian Academy for Erotic Inquiry, where eight individuals have been subjected to telepathic surgery. As the narrator drones on the operation, alternately strange and static scenes are presented which only occasionally bear any relation to the words being spoken.

THE STUFF

1985, 93 mins, ◇ Ⓥ   *Dir* Larry Cohen   US

★ **Stars** Michael Moriarty, Andrea Marcovicci, Paul Sorvino, Scott Bloom, Garrett Morris, Danny Aiello

The Stuff is sci-fi with no hardware but lots of white goo. It's a certified Larry Cohen film that seems to fly right out of the 1950s horror genre. It also has an underlying humor about it, plays around with satirizing fast foods, and cloaks a sly little subtext about people who ingest stuff they know is not good for them.

Film enjoys a larky sense of innocence, some hideous gaping mouths full of a curdling, parasitic menace, and a fey performance by Michael Moriarty as an industrial saboteur who, along with Andrea Marcovicci and little Scott Bloom, track down the scourge of the countryside and the heavies.

It also benefits from a hilarious performance played straight by Paul Sorvino as a self-styled paramilitary nut. The 11-year-old Bloom is appealing, while Garrett Morris as a chocolate cookie mogul and Danny Aiello as Vickers lend flavor in support.

SUPERGIRL

1984, 114 mins, ◇ Ⓥ   *Dir* Jeannot Szwarc   UK

★ **Stars** Faye Dunaway, Helen Slater, Peter O'Toole, Peter Cook, Brenda Vaccaro, Mia Farrow

Supergirl is Kara, Superman's cousin, who journeys from her home on the planet of Argo to Earth to recover the missing Omegahedron Stone, life-force of her world, which has fallen into the clutches of the evil Selena (Faye Dunaway), a power-hungry sorceress.

Landing near an exclusive boarding school for young ladies, Kara quickly adopts the name of Linda Lee and just happens find herself rooming with Lois Lane's kid sister, Lucy (Maureen Teefy).

Rest of pic represents a struggle between the good of Supergirl and the evil of Selena with, as is usually the case, evil being a lot more fun.

Dunaway has a ball as Selena, and her enjoyably over-the-top handling of the part could merit cult attention. She's ably backed by Brenda Vaccaro as her incredulous assistant, and Peter Cook as her sometime lover and math teacher at the girls' school.

Peter O'Toole makes a modest impression as Supergirl's friend and mentor, while Mia Farrow and Simon Ward, as her parents, have even smaller roles than Susannah York and Marlon Brando in the first *Superman*.

Helen Slater is a find: blonde as Supergirl, dark-haired as Linda Lee, she's an appealing young heroine in either guise. Screenplay is filled with witty lines and enjoyable characters, but Jeannot Szwarc's direction is rather flat.

SUPERMAN

1978, 143 mins, ◇ Ⓥ   *Dir* Richard Donner   US

★ **Stars** Marlon Brando, Gene Hackman, Christopher Reeve, Margot Kidder, Ned Beatty, Glenn Ford

Magnify James Bond's extraordinary physical powers while curbing his sex drive and you have the essence of *Superman*, a wonderful, chuckling, preposterously exciting fantasy film.

Forget Marlon Brando who tops the credits. As Superman's father on the doomed planet Krypton, Brando is good but unremarkable.

As both the wholesome man of steel and his bumbling secret identity Clark Kent, Christopher Reeve is excellent. As newswoman Lois Lane, Margot Kidder plays perfectly off both of his personalities.

Tracing the familiar cartoon genesis, film opens with spectacular outer-space effects and the presentation of life on Krypton where nobody believes Papa Brando's warnings of doom. So he and wife Susannah York ship their baby son on his way to Earth.

Striking terra firma, the baby is found by Glenn Ford and Phyllis Thaxter who take him for their own. But the time must ultimately come when Superman's powers for good are revealed to the world and his debut becomes a wild night, beginning with Lois Lane's rescue from a skyscraper, the capture of assorted burglars and the salvation of the president's airplane.

Lurking in wacky palatial splendor in the sewers beneath Park Ave, supercriminal Gene Hackman views this caped arrival as a superthreat befitting his evil genius.

SUPERMAN II

1981, 127 mins, ◇ Ⓥ *Dir* Richard Lester   UK

★ **Stars** Christopher Reeve, Gene Hackman, Margot Kidder, Ned Beatty, Terence Stamp, Sarah Douglas

For all the production halts, setbacks, personnel changeovers and legal wrangling that paved its way to the screen, *Superman II* emerges as a solid, classy, cannily constructed piece of entertainment which gets down to action almost immediately.

Although original plans called for lensing the first two *Superman* features simultaneously, the sequel is reportedly 80% newly shot footage.

The film does an especially good job of picking up the strings of unexplored characters and plot seeds left dangling from the first pic, taking its core plot from the three Kryptonian villains – Terence Stamp, Jack O'Halloran and

Sarah Douglas – briefly glimpsed in the first pic. Here, they're liberated from perpetual imprisonment in a bizarre time-warp by an H-bomb explosion in outer space.

The film builds quickly to a climactic battle between Christopher Reeve and the three supervillains in mid-town Manhatten.

SUPERMAN III

1983, 123 mins, ◇ Ⓥ *Dir* Richard Lester   UK

★ **Stars** Christopher Reeve, Richard Pryor, Robert Vaughn, Annette O'Toole, Annie Ross, Margot Kidder

Superman III emerges as a surprisingly soft-cored disappointment. Putting its emphasis on broad comedy at the expense of ingenious plotting and technical wizardry, it has virtually none of the mythic or cosmic sensibility that marked its predecessors.

The film begins with a hilarious pre-credits sequence in which Richard Pryor, an unemployed 'kitchen technician', decides to embark on a career as a computer programmer. Robert Vaughn, a crooked megalomaniac intent on taking over the world economy, dispatches Pryor to a small compa-

Christopher Reeve as the Man of Steel in the first, and certainly the best, of the Superman sagas.

ny subsid in Smallville, where he programs a weather satellite to destroy Colombia's coffee crop (and make a market-cornering killing for Vaughn).

Foiled by Superman (Christopher Reeve), Pryor uses the computer to concoct an imperfect form of Kryptonite – using cigarette tar to round out the formula. The screenplay opts for the novelty of using the Kryptonite to split the Clark Kent/Superman persona into two bodies, good and evil.

Most of the action relies on explosive pyrotechnics and careening stuntpersons. At the romantic level, the film does paint a nice relationship between Reeve (as Kent) and his onetime crush Annette O'Toole.

SUPERMAN IV THE QUEST FOR PEACE

1987, 89 mins, ◇ ⓥ *Dir* Sidney J. Furie   US

★ *Stars* Christopher Reeve, Gene Hackman, Jackie Cooper, Mariel Hemingway, Jon Cryer, Margot Kidder

Opening sequence shows Superman has picked up the spirit of glasnost as he flies into space to rescue an imperiled cosmonaut and utters his first lines of the picture in Russian.

Better as a board game: The Sword and the Sorcerer features cardboard characters dicing with death.

Superman's newly assumed mission sees him addressing the United Nations to tell the world that he personally is going to remove all nuclear weapons from the face of the earth.

Meanwhile, Lex Luthor (Gene Hackman) has created an evil clone of Superman called Nuclear Man, who wreaks havoc with famous landmarks around the world and does savage battle with the hero on the face of the moon until Superman discovers his nemesis' single flaw.

The earlier films in the series were far from perfect, but at their best they had some flair and agreeable humor, qualities this one sorely lacks. Hackman gets a few laughs, but has less to work with than before, and everyone else seems to be just going through the motions and having less fun doing so.

THE SWORD AND THE SORCERER

1982, 100 mins, ◇ ⓥ *Dir* Albert Pyun   US

★ *Stars* Lee Horsley, Kathleen Beller, Simon MacCorkindale, George Maharis, Richard Lynch, Nina Van Pallandt

Combine beaucoup gore and an atrocity-a-minute action edited in fastpace style. Then, toss in a scantily clad cast of none-too-talented performers mouthing dimwitted dialog and garnish with a touch of medieval gibberish. The result would be something resembling *The Sword and the Sorcerer*.

The plot is needlessly complicated by a truly lackluster script. Stripped to essentials, which the cast often does in this pseudo epic, *Sword* is about the retaking by a group of rag-tag medievalists of a once peaceable kingdom sadistically ruled by an evil knight named Cromwell.

Lee Horsley grins a lot as the leader of the rebels, who turns out to be the long-banished son of the old and virtuous king. Simon MacCorkindale grimaces a good deal as a royal pretender. For trivia fans, Nina Van Pallandt plays the good queen who's dispatched quickly and mercifully since her performance is nothing to boast of.

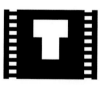

TARANTULA

1955, 80 mins, *Dir* William Alland   US

★ *Stars* John Agar, Mara Corday, Leo G. Carroll, Nestor Paiva, Ross Elliott, Clint Eastwood

A tarantula as big as a barn puts the horror into this well-made program science-fictioner and it is quite credibly staged and played, bringing off the far-fetched premise with a maximum of believability.

Some scientists, stationed near Desert Rock, Ariz, are working on an automatically stabilized nutritional formula that will feed the world's ever-increasing population when the natural food supply becomes too small. Through variously staged circumstances, a tarantula that has been injected with the yet unstabilized formula escapes and, while continuously increasing in size starts living off cattle and humans.

Leo G. Carroll is excellent in his scientist role, while John Agar, young town medico, and Mara Corday carry off the romantic demands very well.

THE TERMINATOR

1984, 108 mins, ◇ Ⓥ *Dir* James Cameron   US

★ **Stars** Arnold Schwarzenegger, Michael Biehn, Linda Hamilton, Paul Winfield, Lance Henriksen, Rick Rossovich

The Terminator is a blazing, cinematic comic book, full of virtuoso moviemaking, terrific momentum, solid performances and a compelling story.

The clever script, co-written by director James Cameron and producer Gale Anne Hurd, opens in a post-holocaust nightmare, A.D. 2029, where brainy machines have crushed most of the human populace. From that point, Arnold Schwarzenegger as the cyborg Terminator is sent back to the present to assassinate a young woman named Sarah Connor (Linda Hamilton) who is, in the context of a soon-to-be-born son and the nuclear war to come, the mother of mankind's salvation.

A human survivor in that black future (Michael Biehn), also drops into 1984 to stop the Terminator and save the woman and the future.

The shotgun-wielding Schwarzenegger is perfectly cast here in a machine-like portrayal that requires only a few lines of dialog.

TERMINATOR 2: JUDGMENT DAY

1991, 108 mins, ◇ Ⓥ *Dir* James Cameron   US

★ **Stars** Arnold Schwarzenegger, Linda Hamilton, Edward Furlong,, Robert Patrick, Earl Boen, Joe Morton

He's back all right, and with enough artillery to virtually ensure action and Arnold Scwarzenegger fans more than their money's worth.

As with *Aliens*, director James Cameron has again taken a first-rate science-fiction film and crafted a sequel that's in some ways more impressive. This time he has managed the trick by bringing two cyborgs back from the future to respectively menace and defend the juvenile John Connor

Arnold Schwarzenegger returns in **Terminator 2**, *this time as the protector of Linda Hamilton (right) and her son.*

(Edward Furlong) – leader of the resistance against machines that rule the war-devestated world of 2029.

The story finds John Connor with foster parents, his mother Sarah (Linda Hamilton) having been captured and committed to an asylum for insisting on the veracity of events pictured in the first film. The machines of the future decide to dispatch a new cyborg to slay him while the human resistance sends its own reprogrammed Terminator back – this one bearing a remarkable resemblance to the evil one that appeared in 1984.

The film's great innovation involves the second cyborg, an advanced model composed of a liquid metal alloy that can metamorphose into the shape of any person it contacts and sprout metal appendages to skewer its victims.

For some, *Terminator 2* will be too much of a good thing, and even the stunning effects become familiar through over exposure, though hardly to the point where one loses appreciation of the remarkable technical wizardry; for the most part, however, its aim is on target.

Script by Cameron and William Wisher at times gets lost amid all the carnage, and the time-bending conundrum is as puzzling as the first time around. Linda Hamilton again offers the sci-fi crowd a fiercely heroic female lead, albeit one who looks like she's been to Madonna's trainer. Other human types generally hold their own against the plentiful pyrotechnics, among them Joe Morton, as the ill-fated scientist, and Furlong.

Stan Winston and the hordes of others involved in the Terminator/T-1000 effects merit Oscar consideration for their contributions which include a major human-robot battle in the future and a dream sequence in which Los Angeles is vaporized.

TESTAMENT

1989, 89 mins, ◇ ⊘ *Dir* Lynne Littman   US

★ *Stars* Jane Alexander, William Devane, Ross Harris, Roxana Zal, Lukas Haas, Kevin Costner

Testament is an exceptionally powerful film dealing with the survivors of a nuclear war. Debuting director Lynne Littman brings an original approach to the grim material.

Based on Carol Amen's magazine story *The Last Testament*, pic depicts a normal, complacent community in the small California town of Hamlin.

The town's calm is shattered when a TV newscast announces that nuclear devices have exploded in New York and on the east coast, with the film proper suddenly going to yellow and whiteout, indicating blasts on the west coast as well. Ham radio operator Henry Abhart (Leon Ames) becomes Hamlin's communications link to the outside world.

Isolated, Hamlin's residents attempt to survive, but within a month over 1,000 people have died from radiation sickness. A young couple (Rebecca De Mornay and Kevin Costner), whose baby has died, drive off together in search of 'a safe place'.

Holding it all together as a tower of strength is actress Jane Alexander as Carol Wetherby, coping with the deaths of

Pest control with a vengeance: the anti-insect squad go in with bug repellant at the ready in **Them!**

Kurt Russell (centre) and other members of a US Antarctic scientific station discuss how to contain **The Thing.**

her family and friends in truly heroic fashion via an understated performance.

THEM!

1954, 93 mins, ⊛ *Dir* Gordon Douglas   US

★ *Stars* James Whitmore, Edmund Gwenn, Joan Weldon, James Arness, Onslow Stevens, Sean McClory

This science-fiction shocker has a well-plotted story, expertly directed and acted in a matter-of-fact style.

The title monsters are mutations caused by radiation from the 1945 detonation of an atomic bomb in the desert. Over the intervening years the tiny insects affected by the lingering radiation have become fantastic creatures, ranging in size from 9 to 12 feet.

James Whitmore, sergeant in the New Mexico State Police, first gets on the track of the incredible beings. Into the picture then come Edmund Gwenn and Joan Weldon, entomologists, and James Arness, FBI man.

With the aid of air force officers Onslow Stevens and Sean McClory, the little group attempts to wipe out the nest of the mutated monsters with flame throwers and gas.

THE THING

1982, 108 mins, ◇ ⊛ *Dir* John Carpenter   US

★ *Stars* Kurt Russell, A. Wilford Brimley, T.K. Carter, David Clennon, Keith David, Richard Dysart

If it's the most vividly guesome monster ever to stalk the screen that audiences crave, then *The Thing* is the thing. On all other levels, however, John Carpenter's remake of Howard Hawks' 1951 sci-fi classic comes as a letdown.

Strong premise has a group of American scientists and researchers posted at an isolated station in Antarctica. A visit to a decimated Norwegian encampment in the vicinity reveals that a space ship, which had remained buried in ice for as many as 100,000 years, has been uncovered, and that no survivors were left to tell what was found.

First manifestation of The Thing arrives in the form of an escaped dog from the Scandinavian camp. It soon becomes clear that The Thing is capable of ingesting, then assuming the bodily form of, any living being.

What the old picture delivered – and what Carpenter has missed – was a sense of intense dread, a fear that the loathed creature might be lurking around any corner or behind any door.

Kurt Russell is the nominal hero, although suicidal attitude adopted towards the end undercuts his status as a centerscreen force.

THE THING (FROM ANOTHER WORLD)

1951, 89 mins, Ⓥ   *Dir* Christian Nyby   US

★ *Stars* Margaret Sheridan, Kenneth Tobey, Robert Cornthwaite, Douglas Spencer, Dewey Martin, James Arness

Strictly offbeat subject matter centers around a weird, outlandish inter-planetary space-hopper (see title) which descends upon earth in what's referred to as a flying saucer.

Christian Nyby's direction sustains a mood of tingling expectancy as a small group of US airmen and scientists stationed near the North Pole learn that a new, mysterious element is playing tricks with their compass-readings, etc. Tension develops effectively as the expedition takes off to reckon with the unearthly intruder. Hawks' production also scores in its depiction of the bleak, snow-swept Arctic region. The background layout, shot in Montana, conveys an air of frigid authenticity.

But the resourcefulness shown in building the plot groundwork is lacking as the yarn gets into full swing. Cast members, headed by Margaret Sheridan and Kenneth Tobey,

fail to communicate any real terror as the 'Thing' makes its appearance and its power potential to destroy the world is revealed.

Screenplay, based on the story *Who Goes There* by John W. Campbell Jr, shows strain in the effort to come up with a cosmic shocker in the name of science-fiction.

THEY LIVE

1988, 93 mins, ◇ Ⓥ   *Dir* John Carpenter   US

★ *Stars* Roddy Piper, Keith David, Meg Foster, George (Buck) Flower, Peter Jason

Conceived on 1950s B-movie sci-fi terms, *They Live* is a fantastically subversive film, a nifty little confection pitting us vs them, the haves vs the have-nots.

Screenplay by 'Frank Armitage' (presumably another Carpenter pseudonym as was 'Martin Quatermass'), based on a Ray Nelson short story [*Eight O'Clock in the Morning*], takes the clever premise that those in control of the global economic power structure are secretly other-worldly aliens.

His leading character, pretentiously named Nada (Roddy Piper), is a heavily muscled working Joe, a wanderer who makes his way to Justiceville, a shantytown settlement for the homeless in the shadows of downtown's skyscrapers.

A group of American scientists discover a creature-in-the-deep-freeze in the original **Thing (From Another World).**

An ambitious vision of a post-world-war future, many of the predictions in 1936's **Things to Come** *were about to.*

A visually stunning evocation of Fifties pulp sci-fi, **This Island Earth** *remains a classic of the genre.*

Nada happens upon some sunglasses which, when worn, reveal a whole alternate existence, in which certain individuals – the ruling class – are instantly recognizable due to their hideously decomposed, skeletal faces.

Nada becomes an outlaw, picking off aliens wherever he can. He seeks an accomplice, first in Meg Foster, who unwillingly rescues him from the police, and then in black co-worker Keith David, another bodybuilder whom he has to fight; seemingly forever; before getting him to try on the glasses.

Pro wrestler Piper comes across quite adequately as the blue collar Everyman, and remainder of the cast is okay.

THINGS TO COME

1936, 97 mins, Ⓥ   *Dir* William Cameron Menzies   UK

★ *Stars* Raymond Massey, Cedric Hardwicke, Edward Chapman, Ralph Richardson, Margaretta Scott, Maurice Braddell

This is England's first $1 million picture. It's an impressive but dull exposition of a bad dream.

H.G. Wells' idea is that in 1946 there will be a new and disastrous world war. It will last for 30 years and, at the end of that time, civilization will be reduced to nothingness, disease having scourged the world. In exile a group of engineers and aviators, however, think things over and decide

that the ravages and wastes of war, properly harnessed and channeled, can be used for the world's salvation.

They take things over, do away with the petty little fascistic countries that have sprung up, do away with their petty little fascistic leaders, and create a new world of steel and glass, radio and television, artificial light and heat. It is all very pictorial, very imaginative, very artificial and it runs on and on.

William Cameron Menzies directs with a firm hand and even manages to inject some power into the fantasy. Where his characters are allowed to live, he sees to it that they also breathe. Georges Perinal's photography is tops. Garlands are also due Harry Zech for trick photography and Ned Mann for special effects.

Raymond Massey is tops as John Cabal, leader of the new world. Ralph Richardson does a splendid job as the Boss, a sort of combo Hitler-Mussolini.

THIS ISLAND EARTH

1955, 87 mins, ◇ Ⓥ   *Dir* Joseph Newman   US

★ *Stars* Jeff Morrow, Faith Domergue, Rex Reason, Lance Fuller, Russell Johnson, Douglas Spencer

Plot motivation in the screenplay is derived from the frantic efforts of the inhabitants of the interstellar planet, Metaluna, to find on Earth a new source of atomic energy. For the accomplishment of this goal, the outstanding scientists in the field have been recruited by a character named Exeter, who has set up a completely-equipped laboratory in Georgia.

One of the most thrilling sequences occurs as huge meteors attack the space ship as it is working its way to Metaluna. Ingeniously-constructed props and equipment, together with strange sound effects also are responsible for furthering interest, which is of the edge-of-the-seat variety during the latter half of the film. For an added fillip, there's a Mutant, half human, half insect, which boards the ship as it escapes from Metaluna.

THX 1138

1971, 88 mins, ◇ ⑦   *Dir* George Lucas   US

★ *Stars* Robert Duvall, Donald Pleasence, Don Pedro Colley, Maggie McOmie, Ian Wolfe, Sid Haig

THX 1138 is a psychedelic science-fiction horror story about some future civilization regimented into computer-programmed slavery.

Film is a feature-length expansion of George Lucas' student film. In that brief form, the story of one man's determination to crash out of his worldly prison was exciting; the

Cybernetic slavery was the theme of George Lucas' pre-Star Wars debut movie THX 1138.

expansion by director-editor Lucas with Walter Murch succeeds in fleshing out the environment, but falls behind in constructing a plot line to sustain interest. Robert Duvall heads cast as the defector after his mate Maggie McOmie is programmed into the cell of Donald Pleasence, a corrupt computer technician. Don Pedro Colley is another fugitive, who helps Duvall reach his freedom.

TIME AFTER TIME

1980, 112 mins, ◇ ⑦   *Dir* Nicholas Meyer   UK

★ *Stars* Malcolm McDowell, David Warner, Mary Steenburgen, Charles Cioffi, Patti D'Arbanville

Time after Time is a delightful, entertaining trifle of a film that shows both the possibilities and limitations of taking liberties with literature and history. Nicholas Meyer has deftly juxtaposed Victorian England and contemporary America in a clever story, irresistible due to the competence of its cast.

H.G. Wells and Jack The Ripper abandon London circa 1893 in Wells' famous time machine. Their arrival in 1979 San Francisco is played for all the inevitable anachronisms, with results that are both witty and pointed.

Thanks to Meyer's astute scripting and direction, and superb performances by Malcolm McDowell as Wells, David Warner as the mythical killer, and Mary Steenburgen as the woman in between, there's plenty of mileage in *Time*.

TIME BANDITS

1981, 110 mins, ◇ ⑦   *Dir* Terry Gilliam   UK

★ *Stars* John Cleese, Sean Connery, Shelley Duvall, Ralph Richardson, David Warner, Michael Palin

When you can count the laughs in a comedy film on the fingers of one hand, it isn't so funny. *Time Bandits*, is a kind of potted history of man, myth and the eternal clash between good and evil as told in the inimitable idiom of Monty Python.

Not that the basic premise is bad, with an English youngster and a group of dwarfs passing through time holes on assignment by the Maker to patch up the shoddier parts of His creation. What results, unfortunately, is a hybrid neither sufficiently hair-raising or comical.

The plot's grand tour ranges from ancient Greece and other parts to the Titanic to the Fortress of Ultimate Darkness, the latter gothic region presided over by a costume-heavy David Warner as one of nine above-title and mostly cameo parts. Of which the funniest, near pic's conclusion, is the Maker Himself as none other than Ralph Richardson in business suit.

John Cleese as Robin Hood, Ian Holm as Napoleon, Sean Connery as a Greek warrior-ruler with a passion for magic, and Michael Palin as a plummy English upperclass type all acquit well enough in the limited circumstances.

John Cleese as Robin Hood in Terry Gilliam's **Time Bandits,** *a Monty Pythonesque romp through history.*

TIME MACHINE

1960, 103 mins, ◇ ⓥ *Dir* George Pal   US

★ *Stars* Rod Taylor, Alan Young, Yvette Mimieux, Sebastian Cabot, Tom Helmore, Whit Bissell

In utilizing contemporary knowledge to update H.G. Wells' durable novel, scenarist David Duncan has brought the work into modern focus. The point-of-view springs properly from 1960 rather than from the turn of the century. The social comment of the original has been historically refined to encompass such plausible eventualities as the physical manifestation of atomic war weapons. But the basic spirit of Wells' work has not been lost.

The film's chief flaw is its somewhat palsied pace. Forging its way through vital initial exposition, it perks to a fascinating peak when the Time Traveller (Rod Taylor) plants himself in his machine and begins his enviable tour of time. His 'visits' to World Wars I, II, and III, and the way in which the passage of time is depicted within these 'local' stops give the picture its most delightful moments.

But things slow down to a walk when Taylor arrives at the year 802,701 and becomes involved generally with a group of tame, antisocial towheads (the Eloi) and specifically with their loveliest and most sociable representative (Yvette Mimieux), with whom he falls in love.

Taylor's performance is a gem of straightforwardness,

with just the proper sensitivity and animation. A standout in support is Alan Young, in a gentle, three-ply role. Mimieux is well cast. Innocent vacancy gleams beautifully in her eyes.

TOTAL RECALL

1990, 109 mins, ◇ ⓥ *Dir* Paul Verhoeven   US

★ *Stars* Arnold Schwarzenegger, Rachel Ticotin, Sharon Stone, Ronny Cox, Michael Ironside, Marshall Bell

Estimates of the cost of this futuristic extravaganza range from $60 to $70 million making it one of the most expensive pics ever made. There are gargantuan sets repping Mars and a futuristic Earth society, grotesque creatures galore, genuinely weird and mostly seamless visual effects, and enough gunshots, grunts and explosions to keep anyone in a high state of nervous exhilaration.

The story is actually a good one, taking off from Phillip K. Dick's celebrated sci-fi tale *We Can Remember It for You Wholesale.*

Arnold Schwarzenegger's character, a working stiff in the year 2084, keeps having these strange nightmares about living on Mars, and it transpires that he once worked in the

Above: *Rod Taylor as the Time Traveller at the controls in* H.G. Wells' **Time Machine.**

Below: *The robot taxi driver rivals Arnie in the solid-jaw stakes, as the latter looks for his memory in* **Total Recall.**

colony as an intelligence agent before rebelling against dictator Ronny Cox. Schwarzenegger had most, but not quite all, of his bad memories erased and was sent to Earth to work on a construction crew, with a sexy but treacherous wife (Sharon Stone).

A visit to a mind-altering travel agency named Rekall Inc. alerts Schwarzenegger to the truth, setting him off on a rampage through Earth and Mars with the help of equally tough female sidekick Rachel Ticotin.

The fierce and unrelenting pace, accompanied by a tongue-in-cheek strain of humor in the roughhouse screenplay, keeps the film moving like a juggernaut.

TROLL

1986, 86 mins, ◇ Ⓥ *Dir* John Buechler   US

★ **Stars** Noah Hathaway, Michael Moriarty, Shelley Hack, Jenny Beck, Sonny Bono

Troll is a predictable, dim-witted premise executed for the most part with surprising style. Horror fantasy of a universe of trolls taking over a San Francisco apartment house is far-fetched even for this genre. Creatures designed by John Buechler, who also directed, are a repulsive assortment of hairy, fanged, evil-looking elves but the plot is pure shlock.

No sooner does the Potter family move into an ordinary looking building than the young daughter (Jenny Beck) is possessed by the troll. Where the film rises above the ordinary is in the domestic scenes when, thanks to her acquired personality, young Beck can flout all the conventions of how a good girl should act. Performances by the kids are convincing.

TROLLENBERG TERROR

1958, 85 mins, Ⓥ *Dir* Quentin Lawrence   UK

★ **Stars** Forrest Tucker, Laurence Payne, Janet Munro, Jennifer Jayne, Warren Mitchell, Andrew Faulds

Based on a successful TV serial by Peter Key, the yarn concerns a creature from outer space secreted in a radioactive cloud on the mountain of Trollenberg in Switzerland. The mysterious disappearance of various climbers brings Forrest Tucker to the scene as a science investigator for UNO. He and a professor at the local observatory set out to solve the problem.

During investigations, two headless corpses are discovered and a couple of ordinary citizens go berserk and turn killers. Main object of the two is Janet Munro who is one of a sister mind-reading act and obviously presents a threat to the sinister visitor.

The taut screenplay extracts the most from the situations and is helped by strong, resourceful acting from a solid cast. Tucker tackles the problem with commendable lack of histrionics and Munro adds considerably to the film's interest with an excellent portrayal of the girl whose talent for

mental telepathy threatens the creature's activities and draws her into great danger.

TRON

1982, 96 mins, ◇ Ⓥ *Dir* Steven Lisberger   US

★ **Stars** Jeff Bridges, Bruce Boxleitner, David Warner, Cindy Morgan, Barnard Hughes, Dan Shor

Tron is loaded with visual delights but falls way short of the mark in story and viewer involvement. Screenwriter-director Steven Lisberger has adequately marshalled a huge force of technicians to deliver the dazzle, but even kids (and specifically computer game freaks) will have a difficult time getting hooked on the situations.

After an awkward 'teaser' intro the story unfolds concisely: computer games designer Kevin Flynn (Jeff Bridges) has had his series of fabulously successful programs stolen by Ed Dillinger (David Warner). Dillinger has consequently risen to position of corporate power and with his Master Control Program (MCP) has increasingly dominated other programmers and users.

Flynn must obtain the evidence stored in computer's memory proving that Dillinger has appropriated his work. His friend Alan Bradley (Bruce Boxleitner) is concurrently working on a watchdog program (called Tron) to thwart the MCP's growing control. The MCP scientifically transforms Flynn into a computer-stored program, bringing the viewer into the parallel world inside the computer.

Computer-generated visuals created by divers hands are impressive but pic's design work and execution consistently lack the warmth and humanity that classical animation provides.

20,000 LEAGUES UNDER THE SEA

1954, 120 mins, ◇ Ⓥ *Dir* Richard Fleischer   US

★ **Stars** Kirk Douglas, James Mason, Paul Lukas, Peter Lorre, Robert J. Wilke, Carleton Young

Walt Disney's production of *20,000 Leagues Under the Sea* is a very special kind of picture, combining photographic ingenuity, imaginative story telling and fiscal daring. Disney went for a bundle (say $5 million in negative costs) in fashioning the Jules Verne classic.

The story of the 'monster' ship *Nautilus*, astounding as it may be, is so astutely developed that the audience immediately accepts its part on the excursion through Captain Nemo's underseas realm.

James Mason is the captain, a genius who had fashioned and guides the out-of-this-world craft. Kirk Douglas is a free-wheeling, roguish harpoon artist. Paul Lukas is a kind and gentle man of science and Peter Lorre is Lukas' fretting apprentice.

But it is the production itself that is the star. Technical skill was lavished in fashioning the fabulous *Nautilus* with its exquisitely appointed interior. The underwater lensing is remarkable on a number of counts, among them being the special designing of aqua-lungs and other equipment to match Verne's own illustrations.

Story opens in San Francisco where maritime men have been terrorized by reports of a monstrous denizen of the seas which has been sinking their ships. An armed frigate sets out in pursuit and is itself destroyed, with Lukas, Douglas and Lorre the survivors.

TWILIGHT ZONE THE MOVIE

1983, 102 mins, ◇ Ⓥ *Dir* John Landis, Steven Spielberg, Joe Dante, George Miller   US

★ *Stars* Dan Aykroyd, Albert Brooks, Vic Morrow, Scatman Crothers, Kathleen Quinlan, John Lithgow

Twilight Zone, feature film spinoff from Rod Serling's perennially popular 1960s TV series, plays much like a traditional vaudeville card, what with its tantalizing teaser opening followed by three sketches of increasing quality, all building up to a socko headline act.

Pic consists of prolog by John Landis as well as vignettes, none running any longer than original TV episodes,

by Landis, Steven Spielberg, Joe Dante and George Miller. Dante and Miller manage to shine the brightest in this context.

Landis gets things off to a wonderful start with a comic prolog starring Dan Aykroyd and Albert Brooks.

Landis' principal episode, however, is a downbeat, one-dimensional fable about racial and religious intolerance. An embittered, middle-aged man who has just been passed over for a job promotion, Vic Morrow sports a torrent of racial epithets aimed at Jews, Blacks and Orientals while drinking with buddies at a bar. Upon exiting, he finds himself in Nazi-occupied Paris as a suspected Jew on the run from the Gestapo.

This is the only sequence in the film not derived from an actual TV episode, although it does bear a thematic resemblance to a 1961 installment titled *A Quality of Mercy*.

Spielberg's entry is the most down-to-earth of all the stories. In a retirement home filled with oldsters living in the past, spry Scatman Crothers encourages various residents to think young and, in organizing a game of kick the can, actually transforms them into their childhood selves again.

Most bizarre contribution comes from Dante. Outsider Kathleen Quinlan enters the Twilight Zone courtesy of little Jeremy Licht, who lords it over a Looney-Tune household by virtue of his power to will anything into existence except happiness.

But wisely, the best has been saved for last. Miller's re-working of *Nightmare at 20,000 Feet*, about a man, played by John Lithgow, who sees a gremlin tearing up one of the engines on the wing of an airplane, is electrifying from beginning to end.

Keir Dullea gropes for his sanity inside the memory bank of HAL, the renegade computer of 2001: A Space Odyssey.

2001: A SPACE ODYSSEY

1968, 160 mins, ◇ Ⓥ *Dir* Stanley Kubrick   UK

★ *Stars* Keir Dullea, Gary Lockwood, William Sylvester, Daniel Richter, Douglas Rain, Leonard Rossiter

When Stanley Kubrick and science-fiction specialist Arthur C. Clarke first conceived the idea of making a Cinerama film, neither had any idea that it would run into a project of several years.

A major achievement in cinematography and special effects, *2001* lacks dramatic appeal and only conveys suspense after the halfway mark; Kubrick must receive all the praise – and take all the blame.

The plot, so-called, uses up almost two hours in exposition of scientific advances in space travel and communications, before anything happens.

The little humor is provided by introducing well-known commercial names which are presumably still operational during the space age – the Orbiter Hilton hotel and Pan Am space ships.

Keir Dullea and Gary Lockwood, as the two principal astronauts, are not introduced until well along in the film. Their complete lack of emotion becomes rather implausible during scenes where they discuss the villainy of Hal, the talking computer.

Kubrick and Clarke have kept dialog to a minimum, frequently inserting lengthy passages where everything is told visually. The tremendous centrifuge which makes up the principal set (in which the two astronauts live and travel) reportedly cost $750,000 and looks every bit of it.

2010

1984, 114 mins, ◇ Ⓥ *Dir* Peter Hyams   US

★ *Stars* Roy Scheider, John Lithgow, Helen Mirren, Bob Balaban, Keir Dullea, Douglas Rain

As the title proclaims, *2010* begins nine years after something went wrong with the Jupiter voyage of Discovery. On earth, politicians have brought the US and Russia to the brink of war, but their scientists have united in a venture to return to Jupiter to seek an answer to Discovery's fate and the significance of the huge black monolith that orbits near it.

American crew is headed by Roy Scheider, John Lithgow and Bob Balaban. The Soviets want them along mainly for their understanding of HAL 9000, whose mutiny remains unexplained. If revived in the salvage effort, can HAL still be trusted?

In director Peter Hyams' hands, the HAL mystery is the most satisfying substance of the film and is handled the best. Unfortunately, it lies amid a hodge-podge of other bits and pieces.

ULYSSES

1954, 104 mins, ◇ Ⓥ *Dir* Mario Camerini   ITALY

★ *Stars* Kirk Douglas, Silvana Mangano, Anthony Quinn, Rossana Podesta, Jaques Dumesnil

A lot, perhaps too much, money went into the making of *Ulysses*, but expense shows. Besides the epic Homeric peg, pic has an internationally balanced cast, with Yank, French and Italian elements predominant.

Only a few of the w.k. Homeric episodes have been included in the already lengthy pic, and are told in flashback form as remembered by the hero. Featured are his love for Nausicaa; the cave of Polyphemus, the one-eyed monster; the Siren Rocks; the visit to Circe's Island cave and the return to Penelope. But material covered makes for plenty of action, dominated by a virile performance by Kirk Douglas.

Others include co-star Silvana Mangano, a looker, as both Circe and Penelope, but unfortunately limited by both parts to expressing monotonous unhappiness until the finale. Anthony Quinn handles his bits well. For a spectacle, the pic runs too many closeups, with longish stretches of dialog between the two principals, or soliloquized.

Above: *A team of civilians and submariners discuss tactics in* Voyage to the Bottom of the Sea.

VILLAGE OF THE DAMNED

1960, 77 mins, Ⓥ   *Dir* Wolf Rilla   UK

★ *Stars* George Sanders, Barbara Shelley, Martin Stephens, Michael Gwynn, Laurence Naismith

Plot kicks around what is not an uninteresting idea. A little British village comes under the spell of some strange, supernatural force which first puts everybody out for the count. Then the villagers come to and find that every woman capable of being pregnant is.

The major snag is that all the children are little monsters. They all look alike – fair haired, unblinking stare and with intellects the equivalent of adults, plus the unnerving knack of mental telepathy. George Sanders, a physicist, is intimately involved, since his own wife is the mother of the

Left: *Barbara Shelley looks suitably suspicious of her other-wordly offspring in* Village of the Damned.

leader of the little gang of abnormal moppets. Sanders decides to probe the mystery.

If there had happened to be any hint of why this remarkable business should have occurred, the film [from the novel *Midwich Cuckoos* by John Wyndham] would have been slightly more plausible. As it is, this just tapers off from a taut beginning into soggy melodrama. Wolf Rilla's direction is adequate, but no more.

VOYAGE TO THE BOTTOM OF THE SEA

1961, 105 mins, ◇ Ⓥ   *Dir* Irwin Allen   US

★ *Stars* Walter Pidgeon, Joan Fontaine, Barbara Eden, Peter Lorre, Michael Ansara, Frankie Avalon

Voyage is a crescendo of mounting jeopardy, an effervescent adventure in an anything-but-Pacific Ocean.

The way the story goes, this brilliant admiral (Walter Pidgeon), commander of a marvelous atomic sub that resembles a smiling Moby Dick, devises a scheme to save mankind when life on earth is suddenly threatened by a girdle of fire caused when the Van Allen Belt of Radiation encircling the globe goes berserk and erupts. Trouble is mankind does not seem to want to be saved and unable to contact the US prez (golfing?), skipper Pidgeon heads for a spot near the Marianas where he plans to orbit a Polaris and explode the heavenly blaze out into space.

Actually the title is somewhat misleading. Customers who expect a kind of advanced course in oceanography will discover only an occasional giant squid and a lot of rubbery vegetation. For the most part, *The Bottom* of director Irwin

Allen's *Sea* is merely the setting for the kind of emotional calisthenics that might just as easily break out 100 feet from the tip of Mount Everest.

The acting is generally capable, about the best it can be under the trying dramatic circumstances.

THE WAR GAME

1966, 50 mins, ⚫ *Dir* Peter Watkins   UK

The War Game was originally made by BBC-TV for showing on TV, but corporation brass had second thoughts after it had been completed, decided it was unsuitable for mass audiences, and ordered it to be kept off the airwaves. As a result of political and press agitation, it was eventually agreed to make it available for theatrical release through the British Film Institute.

A wholly imaginary picture of what could happen immediately before, during and after a nuclear attack on Britain, *The War Game* is grim, gruesome, horrific and realistic. It is not a pleasant picture to watch, but yet it is one that needs to be shown as widely as possible.

The attack itself is predictably grim, but the most telling part is the aftermath of the bomb – the severely burned are killed off and their bodies burned, and looters face the firing squad.

Watkins, who left the BBC in protest when it was banned, does an excellent and imaginative job, based on considerable research.

WARLOCK

1989, 102 mins, ◇ ⓥ *Dir* Steve Miner   US

★ **Stars** Richard E. Grant, Julian Sands, Lori Singer, Kevin O'Brien, Richard Kuse

Warlock is an attempt to concoct a pic from a pinch of occult chiller, a dash of fantasy thriller and a splash of 'stalk 'n' slash'. But what could have been a heady brew falls short, despite some gusto thesping from Richard E. Grant and Lori Singer.

Pic opens in the Massachusetts Bay colony in 1691 where a contemptuous warlock (Julian Sands) is being readied for execution. But with a bit of nifty hocus-pocus, both he and witch-hunter Richard E. Grant are sent to 1988 LA.

Sands soon gets back to his nasty habits – including chopping off a finger, gouging out eyes and skinning a child – as he pursues the magical book the *Grand Grimoire*. Waitress Lori Singer meets Sands when he crashes through a window into her house. After he puts an ageing spell on her, she teams up with Grant to try to kill the warlock.

Julian Sands puts the evil eye on the audience before going berserk in Beverly Hills in **Warlock***.*

Director Steve Miner directs ably but doesn't pull away from some of the horror cliches.

WARLORDS OF ATLANTIS

1978, 96 mins, ◇ ⓥ *Dir* Kevin Connor   UK

★ **Stars** Doug McClure, Peter Gilmore, Shane Rimmer, Lea Brodie, Michael Gothard, Cyd Charisse

In *Warlords of Atlantis*, Doug McClure and several other earthlings suffer a close encounter with Cyd Charisse and Daniel Massey who rule over the legendary lost city. More terrifying are their brushes with various species of marine monsters on periodic rampages. And a good thing, too, in an otherwise skimpy reworking of the hoary Atlantis legend.

Donald Bisset and Peter Gilmore are appealing as a British father-son scientific team in quest of Atlantis. McClure is the Yank who made the diving bell that plumbs the sea and implausibly manages to resurface.

The one not inconsiderable virtue of the script is that it keeps the pot boiling. Direction by Kevin Connor and the editing keep the eye-filling pace brisk. The cliched characters are played in workmanlike fashion by all hands.

THE WAR OF THE WORLDS

1953, 85 mins, ◇ Ⓥ *Dir* Byron Haskin   US

★ *Stars* Gene Barry, Ann Robinson, Les Tremayne, Lewis Martin, Bob Cornthwaite

War of the Worlds is a socko science-fiction feature, as fearsome as a film as was the Orson Welles 1938 radio interpretation of the H.G. Wells novel. Gene Barry, as a scientist, is the principal in this story of an invasion of the earth by weird, spider-like characters from Mars, against whom the world's most potent weapons, even the atom bomb are of no avail.

Into this setup, the special effects group headed by Gordon Jennings loosens a reign of screen terror, of futile defense, demolished cities, charred landscapes and people burned to ashes by the invaders' weapons.

While following closely the plot laid down in Wells' novel, the film transfers the first invasion to a small town in Southern California. What is believed to be a huge meteor lands near a small town but it turns out to be a Martian machine that raises itself on pulsating beams and promptly turns deadly heatwaves on humans, buildings and anything else that comes within range.

In the siege of terror, the story finds opportunity to develop a logical love story between Barry and Ann Robinson. Both are good and others seen to advantage include Les Tremayne as a general; Lewis Martin, a pastor who faces the invaders with a prayer and is struck down. An ominous commentary is spoken by Cedric Hardwicke.

WEIRD SCIENCE

1985, 94 mins, ◇ Ⓥ *Dir* John Hughes   US

★ *Stars* Anthony Michael Hall, Kelly LeBrock, Ilan Mitchell-Smith, Bill Paxton, Suzanne Snyder, Robert Downey

Starting with the delectable premise of two high school nerds who create a woman through some inexplicable computer hocus-pocus, *Weird Science* veers off into a typical coming-of-age saga without exploring any of the psychological territory it lightly sails over in the early going.

Machines from Mars which can withstand man's most potent weapons attack Earth in **The War of the Worlds.**

Paramount Presents "THE WAR OF THE WORLDS" Color by TECHNICOLOR CERT. X

Produced by George Pal   Directed by Byron Haskin   Screenplay by Barre Lyndon   Based on the Novel by H. G. Wells.
These stills are copyright. They must not be traded, resold, given away or subleased. They should be returned to Paramount Film Service after exhibition.

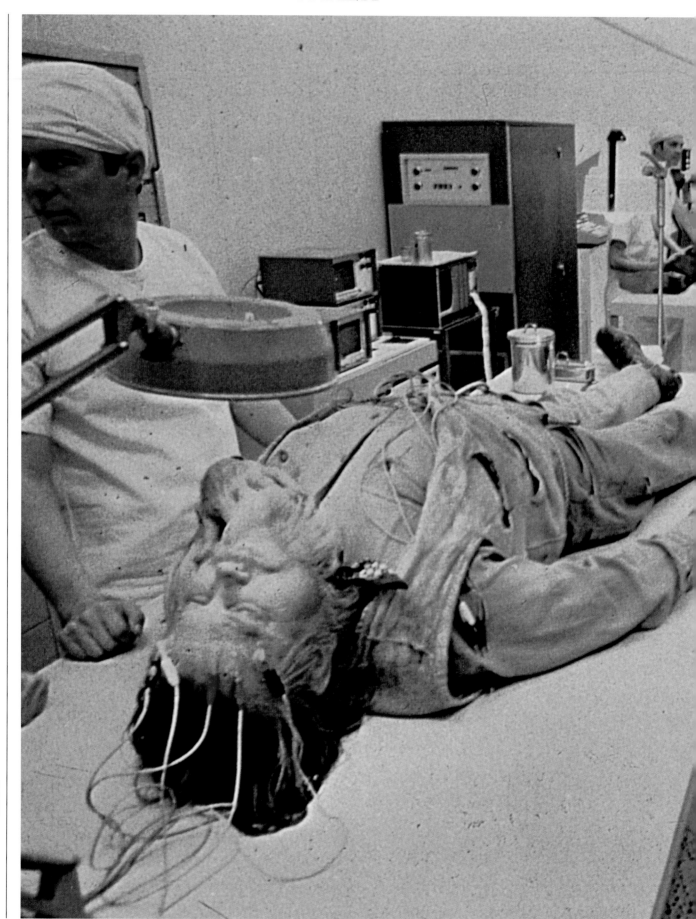

Technicians repair the automated robots from **Westworld,**
a believable future with simulated participation vacations.

Helplessly horny chums Gary (Anthony Michael Hall)
and Wyatt (Ilan Mitchell-Smith), in an act of creative frustra-
tion, put their brains together and create the answer to their
fantasies – the beautiful and very available Lisa (Kelly
LeBrock). The trouble is the boys hardly use her.

Although clearly not grounded in reality, the film really goes nowhere with its central conceit, opting instead for a
more ordinary approach . Director John Hughes never capi-
talizes on the idea that Lisa is a creation of 15-year-old psyches or examines the intriguing question of who controls
whom in this relationship.

Hughes' true gift is at capturing the naturalistic
rhythms and interaction between the boys with a great ear
for dialog. LeBrock is just right as the film's calm but com-
manding center.

WELCOME TO BLOOD CITY

1977, 96 mins, ◇ ⑰ *Dir* Peter Sasdy   UK, CANADA

★ *Stars* Jack Palance, Keir Dullea, Samantha Eggar, Barry
Morse, Hollis McLaren, Chris Wiggins

An anonymous totalitarian organization kidnaps Keir Dullea.
Via computer electronics, he is mentally transported to a
fantasized oater settlement (Blood City) where a person's
status accrues according to the number of people he/she
can murder. Sheriff Jack Palance is classified as Immortal,
having 20 killings to his score.

Dullea's progress through the city is monitored by program technicians Samantha Eggar (who also inexplicably
lives in Blood City) and John Evans.

Although the film's initial conception may have held
traces of intelligence, swiss-cheese script strains coherence
and interest with each development. Consequently, neither
in their interdependence or individuality do the film's sci-fi
or western elements emerge as generically satisfying.

WESTWORLD

1973, 88 mins, ◇ ⑰ *Dir* Michael Crichton   US

★ *Stars* Yul Brynner, Richard Benjamin, James Brolin, Alan
Oppenheimer, Victoria Shaw, Dick Van Patten

Westworld is an excellent film, which combines solid
entertainment, chilling topicality, and superbly intelligent
serio-comic story values. Michael Crichton's original script is
as superior as his direction.

Crichton's Westworld is one of three gigantic theme
parks built in what is left of the American outdoors; the others are 'Romanworld' and 'Medievalworld'. For $1,000 a day,
flown in tourists may indulge their highest and lowest ap-
petities. Automated robots move about as real people. These

automatons may be raped, shot to death, befriended, betrayed, etc. They never strike back.

To this world come Richard Benjamin and James Brolin. They have picked the western-themed park, where they switch to levis, pack revolvers and live out the screen life depicted by John Wayne, Clint Eastwood, and other actioner stars. Yul Brynner plays a black-clothed bad guy whom Benjamin kills in a saloon confrontation. All the while supervisor Alan Oppenheimer oversees the entire world and its creatures.

But suddenly things begin to go wrong. An unidentified computer casualty begins to spread like a plague. The automatons strike back.

WHEN WORLDS COLLIDE

1951, 81 mins, ◇ ⓥ *Dir* Rudolph Mate   US

★ **Stars** Richard Derr, Barbara Rush, Peter Hanson, John Hoyt, Larry Keating, Judith Ames

Top honors for this inter-planetary fantasy rest with the cameramen and special effects technicians rather than with performances of the non-name cast. Process photography and optical illusions are done with an imaginativeness that vicariously sweeps the spectator into space.

Story is predicated upon the findings of a scientist (Hayden Rorke) that a planet, Zyra, will pass so close to the earth a year hence that oceans will be pulled from their beds. Moreover, 19 days after this catastrophe, the star, Bellus, will collide with whatever remains of the world.

Unfortunately, scripter Sydney Boehm who fashioned the screenplay [from a novel by Edwin Balmer and Philip Wylie], chose to work in a romance between Barbara Rush, daughter of astronomer Larry Keating, and Richard Derr, a plane pilot. His love rival is Peter Hanson, a doctor.

Departure, actual flight and landing upon Zyra represent the highpoint of the picture. Somewhat of a puzzle, however, is the fact that although the ship lands upon an ice-covered valley, its occupants step out into a verdant paradise when opening the craft's door.

WHO?

1974, 93 mins, ◇ *Dir* Jack Gold   UK, W. GERMANY

★ **Stars** Elliott Gould, Trevor Howard, Joe Bova, Ed Grover, James Noble, Lyndon Brook

Adapted from Algis Budrys' novel by British playwright John Gould, *Who?* is an action-espionage thriller examining, from a science-fiction perspective, the nature of identity.

Joe Bova gives a beautiful, underplayed performance as diminutive US scientist Martino, whose face and arm are remade in metal after an accident in Berlin. The film's mystery-suspense plot derives from iterated flashbacks showing Martino grilled and/or indoctrinated by East German intelligence officer Azarin (Trevor Howard).

Once back in the US, Martino is subjected to gruelling questioning and investigation by FBI operative Rogers (Elliott Gould) to check his new security clearance for continuing a top secret research project in Florida. Gould examines the reactions of Martino's old associates to his transformed, robot-like appearance.

Gould brings humor to the assignment. Howard is seen only in the flashbacks.

THE WITCHES

1990, 92 mins, ◇ ⓥ *Dir* Nicolas Roeg   US

★ **Stars** Anjelica Houston, Mai Zetterling, Jasen Fisher, Rowan Atkinson, Bill Paterson

The wizardry of Jim Henson's Creature Shop and a superbly over-the-top performance by Angelica Huston gives *The Witches* a good deal of charm and enjoyment.

Pic opens in Norway where grandmother Helga (Mai Zetterling) is telling her nine-year-old grandson Luke (Jasen Fisher) about witches and their wicked ways. His parents die in a car crash, and Luke and grandmother travel to England for a holiday.

They go to a stark Cornish hotel. Also checking in is the annual ladies meeting of the Royal Society for the Prevention of Cruelty to Children; in actual fact a meeting of the British witches, due to be addressed by the Grand High Witch, Huston. Young Luke accidentally overhears the meeting where Huston announces her grand plan to feed poisoned chocolate to all British children, which will turn them into mice.

In a tight black dress and vampish haircut, Huston seems to enjoy herself in her role as the evil chief witch, and the pic seems to be merely plodding along until she arrives on the scene.

THE WORLD, THE FLESH AND THE DEVIL

1959, 95 mins, *Dir* Ranald MacDougall   US

★ **Stars** Harry Belafonte, Inger Stevens, Mel Ferrer

This is a provocative three-character story dealing with some pertinent issues (racism, atomic destruction) in a frame of suspense melodrama. Ranald MacDougall, who directed his own screenplay (based on an ancient novel by M.P. Shiel), leaves a few holes in his story, but deliberately.

Harry Belafonte is a coal miner who fights his way out of a wrecked Pennsylvania shaft to find himself apparently alone in a devastated world. After about a third of the film, Inger Stevens turns up, spared because she was in a decompression chamber when the bombs burst. Near the ending, in the last half-hour or so, Mel Ferrer arrives in a small power boat from a fishing expedition.

Although overall the film is engrossing, it gets curiously less effective as each additional survivor turns up. When Belafonte is entirely alone on the screen for the first one-third of the film, and virtually alone for the first half, the semi-documentary style keeps *The World, The Flesh And The Devil* a crisp and credible film.

It is not clear in the relationship between Belafonte and Stevens whether they are kept apart by her prejudice or his unfounded fear that such an attitude might exist. Ferrer's character is unsatisfying. He seems to be a racist of sorts, but how virulent isn't entirely clarified.

MacDougall shot a great deal of the film in Manhattan, and the realism (and the pains taken to achieve it) pay off. New Yorkers might complain that their geography is a little mixed up, but this is of small consequence.

visit a party where the women are nude to him.

Things get worse as he kills a friend inadvertently, forcing the doctor to hide out in a carnival as a mindreader. A girl who believes in him tries to help and they go off to work on some antidote.

There are many interesting comic, dramatic and philosophical ideas touched on but treated only on the surface. However, director Roger Corman keeps this moving and Ray Milland is competent as the doomed man. Special effects on his prism-eye world, called Spectarama, are good if sometimes repetitive.

X – THE MAN WITH X-RAY EYES

1963, 80 mins, ◇ Ⓥ *Dir* Roger Corman   US

★ *Stars* Ray Milland, Diana Van Der Vlis, Harold J. Stone, Don Rickles, John Hoyt

Basically it's the plot where the scientist tampers with the unknown and is severely punished in the end. Ray Milland is a doctor who has devised a drug that he thinks will allow men's eyes to see infinitely more.

He tries it on himself when he is refused a grant to continue experiments on animals. He at first is put out of commission by a blinding light but then can see inside human tissue and through clothes. This permits him to

ZARDOZ

1974, 104 mins, ◇ Ⓥ *Dir* John Boorman   UK

★ *Stars* Sean Connery, Charlotte Rampling, Sara Kestelman, John Alderton, Sally Ann Newton, Niall Buggy

Zardoz is a futuristic, metaphysical and anthropological drama testing John Boorman in three creative areas. The results: direction, good; script, a brilliant premise which unfortunately washes out in climactic sound and fury; and

Ray Milland stares out the cameraman in the Roger Corman cult creepy **X - The Man With X-Ray Eyes.**

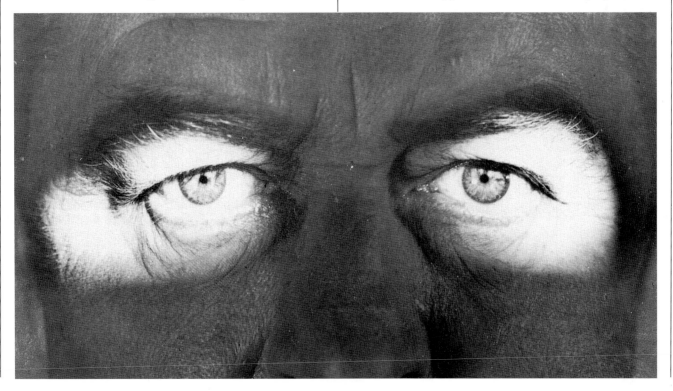

Sean Connery plots a one-man revolution in the weird world of John Boorman's Zardoz.

production, outstanding, particularly special visual effects which belie the film's modest cost. Sean Connery heads the cast as a 23rd-century Adam.

The story, set in 2293, postulates a world society which this century's runaway technology forced into being. The highest order beings are an elitist group of effete aesthetics, eternally youthful on a spiritual plane. Connery rises from the lower ranks to overthrow the new order and recycle mankind into its older pattern.

Connery manifests well the brooding duality of man's nature, emerging from mechanical breeding to eventually tear down the system that created him.